Critical Acclaim for the first book in the How It Works series,

PC Computing How Computers Work

"A 'real' book, and quite a handsome one...The artwork, by Mr. Timothy Edward Downs, is striking and informative, and the text by Mr. White, executive editor of [*PC/Computing*] is very lucid."

—L.R. Shannon, *New York Times*

"...a magnificently seamless integration of text and graphics that makes the complicated physics of the personal computer seem as obvious as gravity. When a book really pleases you—and this one does—there's a tendency to gush, so let's put it this way: I haven't seen any better explanations written (including my own) of how a PC works and why."

—Larry Blasko, *The Associated Press*

"If you're curious but fear computerese might get in the way, this book's the answer...it's an accessible, informative introduction that spreads everything out for logical inspection. Readers will come away knowing not only what everything looks like but also what it does."

—Stephanie Zvirin, *Booklist*

Critical Acclaim for John Rizzo's *MacUser Guide to Connectivity*

"If you want to build bridges across platforms or operating systems, Rizzo's *MacUser Guide to Connectivity* is a good place to start."

—Carol Holzberg, *Reseller World*

HOW
MACS WORK

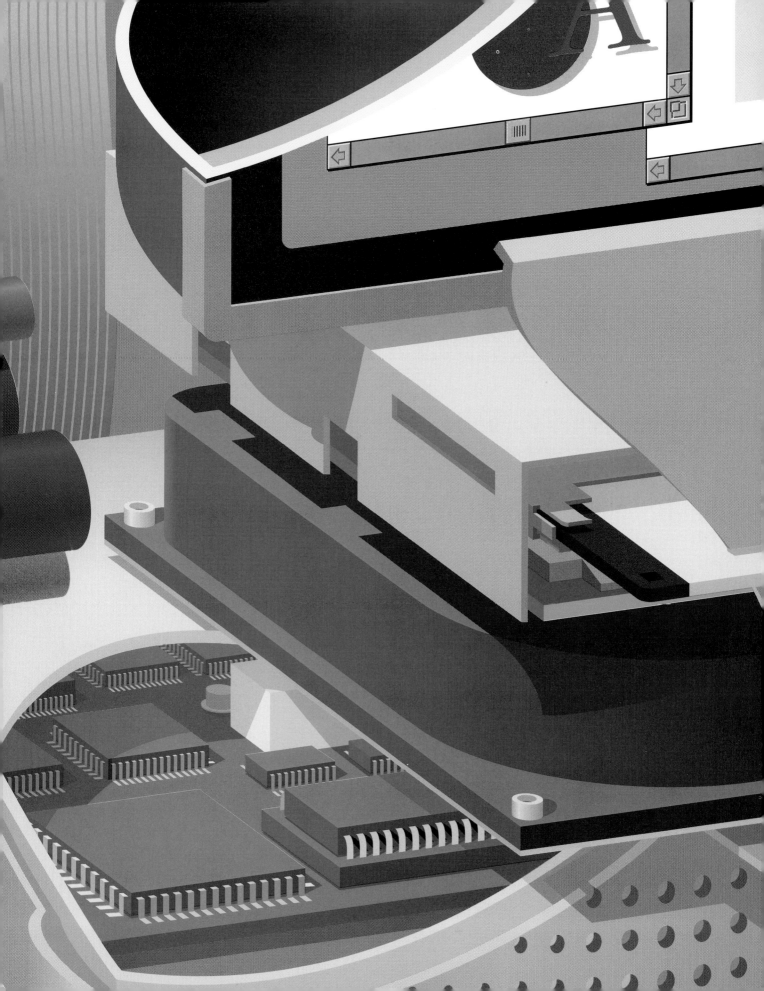

HOW
MACS WORK

JOHN RIZZO
AND K. DANIEL CLARK

Ziff-Davis Press
Emeryville, California

Development Editors	Jeff Green and Valerie Haynes Perry
Copy Editor	Noelle Graney
Technical Reviewer	Gregory Wasson
Project Coordinator	Kim Haglund
Proofreader	Cort Day
Cover Illustrator	K. Daniel Clark
Cover Designer	Carrie English
Series Book Designer	Carrie English
Illustrator	K. Daniel Clark
Word Processors	Howard Blechman, Cat Haglund, Allison Levin
Layout Artist	Bruce Lundquist
Digital Prepress Specialist	Joe Schneider
Indexer	Mark Kmetzko

Ziff-Davis Press books are produced on a Macintosh computer system with the following applications: FrameMaker®, Microsoft® Word, QuarkXPress®, Adobe Illustrator®, Adobe Photoshop®, Adobe Streamline™, MacLink®Plus, Aldus® FreeHand™, Gryphon Morph, Collage Plus™.

Ziff-Davis Press
5903 Christie Avenue
Emeryville, CA 94608

ISBN 1-56276-146-3

Manufactured in the United States of America

10 9 8 7 6 5 4 3 2 1

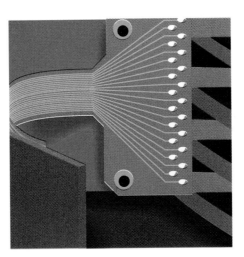

For my wife, Christine, who takes time
out from her own work to help and
support me with mine.

John Rizzo

To Nancy and Ken, Therese, Katie, Patty,
Tony, Tony, and Nick. Their teaching, love,
and support make life wonderful.

K. Daniel Clark

PART 4

Disk Storage
94

PART 1

Inside the Mac
1

PART 3

CPU and Memory
56

PART 2

The System
22

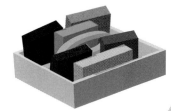

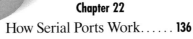

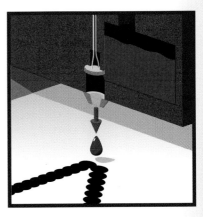

When I bought my first Macintosh, I had a hunch that this product was going to change the face of computing. Before the Mac, computers were not very easy to use. You had to master sets of complex commands that were meaningless to most. The Mac put computing in the hands of people who might not have ventured into computing.

For a few years, those "other" computer users scoffed at us Mac owners. Real computer users didn't use mice, windows, and pictures. Of course, any computer today worth its weight in floppy disks uses mice, windows, and pictures. And, the term "user friendly," first applied to the Macintosh, has become part of our general vocabulary and is used to describe all sorts of things—camcorders, public buildings, and even packaging.

The Mac makes computing easy because it's a tightly integrated system of software and hardware designed to hide the complexities of a computer. But being in the dark isn't always a good thing. There have been times when something went wrong when I wished I had a resource handy that explained what was going on inside my Mac. Something graphical, something easy to understand, from people who know the Mac inside and out. John Rizzo and Dan Clark's *How Macs Work* is just that book.

John knows more than a little about what goes on inside the Mac. He's been a part of the Mac scene ever since the first machine was unveiled and has been writing and commenting on the world of the Macintosh for six years. John has always been an advocate of making computer technology accessible, and he's proven with this book that you don't need a computer science degree to understand it. He and Dan Clark, one of the industry's top electronic illustrators, have combined their considerable talents and have turned complex engineering concepts into professionally crafted illustrations that combine technical comprehensiveness with visual depth. The concept behind the book is inspired by the How It Works series that ran as part of the popular *MacUser* hardware feature section for many years. John and Dan worked on many of those features, and *How Macs Work* picks up where those articles left off.

How Macs Work has something for every Mac user. It covers every aspect of Macintosh technology, from RAM and ROM to disk drives and peripherals. Each chapter of this book is like seeing a mystery unfold before your eyes. Ever wonder what happens when you slip a floppy disk into the drive? Chapter 15 shows it all, including thoughtful, lucidly written text to guide you through each illustration. And these illustrations are nothing short of exquisite. But don't take my word for it—let John and Dan's explanation of LCD displays in Chapter 26 convince you.

How Macs Work is a visual and technical treat and an excellent addition to any Mac user's library.

Maggie Canon
Editor-in-chief, *MacUser*

Many thanks to Jeff Green, who edited most of this book and helped us conceptualize much of it. We were lucky to experience his enthusiasm for his work, even when it meant more work for us. Also thanks to Valerie Haynes Perry, the editor who helped us wrap up this project, and to Kim Haglund, for helping with the logistics of the art.

Thanks to the many people at Apple Computer who were helpful in answering obscure questions and pointing us in the right direction. We are also grateful to *MacUser* magazine, for the use of its resources, and to its staff, for constantly demanding perfection. Dan is grateful to Mike Yapp for showing him how to draw from the inside, and Lisa Orsini, for teaching him the language of illustration.

There are several excellent sources of technical illustration that we found indispensable as resources. For the official word on Mac programming and hardware, there is no substitute for the Inside Macintosh series and *The Guide to the Macintosh Family Hardware*, both by Apple Corp. Also helpful for anyone interested in software development on the Mac are *How to Write Macintosh Software* by Scott Knaster, and *Macintosh Programming Secrets* by Scott Knaster and Keith Rollin. These were the first books on programming that John actually enjoyed reading. *Adobe PostScript Language Reference Manual*, second edition, contains everything you need to know for programming and developing PostScript.

Ever wonder what happens when you pull down a menu? Insert a floppy disk? Move a mouse? Ever wonder what makes a Mac so easy to use? The answer lies behind the windows, inside the microchips, and among the microscopic particles that make up the bits and bytes we call data. A Mac is more than windows and a mouse. It's a complex system of interrelated circuits and software, designed symbiotically from the ground up to work together to make the Mac do what you want it to.

The Mac has now been around for ten years, during which time it has traveled almost everywhere on earth, and even aboard the space shuttle. The Mac has changed much during that time, and is still evolving into more powerful and flexible forms. Yet, even with new processors and parts, today's Macs can still run much of the software designed a decade ago. This has to do with the basic philosophy of the Mac design, which is a constant. It's a philosophy of modular integration, and of enabling a user to do his or her own work instead of the work of learning a computer system. The user interface is not something slapped on top of the system, but is an integral part of the system itself. We follow this philosophy throughout this book.

How Macs Work is not a technical manual. We have tried to make this book Mac-like. Through communicating in a mostly graphical form, we have endeavored to create an easy-to-use book. The text is written in conversational language, and a conscious effort has been made to avoid acronyms and technical jargon whenever possible. However, this book is full of information, covering every aspect of the Macintosh, from ROM to peripherals. It goes into many details never before presented in layperson's terms. Concepts of software and hardware that are often presented in two different technical languages have been integrated together here. We feel you can't separate the two, because that is how Macs work.

You may want to start with Part 1, a look inside the different types of Macs and the parts that make them up. From here you can jump to an area that interests you, much like you point and click on the Mac screen. (Unfortunately, you'll have to turn the pages yourself.) If you read this book linearly, you'll first find the core Mac processes, and gradually move out toward the peripherals outside of the Mac case. We end, appropriately, with a chapter on the desktop publishing process that made the Mac popular and created this book.

INSIDE THE MAC

CONTENTS

OVERVIEW

UPON FIRST GLANCE, the inside of a Macintosh looks like a mysterious jumble of silicon, metal, and plastic. Microscopic electronic circuits, macroscopic mechanical subsystems, and cabling work together to provide the icons and menus of the Mac desktop as well as the processing power behind it. The fact that many Mac users have never seen these components should not be surprising—the Mac is designed to let you do everything you need to from the keyboard, mouse, and exterior ports. So, unless you are upgrading or repairing a Mac, there is little reason to open one up. There are no switches to set, and most of the internal hardware can be reconfigured through software with the click of a mouse. Plug in, turn on, and tune in.

The several dozen models of Macs have all evolved from a common ancestor, the original 128K Mac, and all contain a basic set of core components in one form or another. The central component of any personal computer is the *logic board.* The Mac's logic board contains most of the thinking parts of a Mac, including the central processing unit (CPU), random-access memory (RAM), and the operating system, which is built into a microchip called read-only memory (ROM). The logic board also contains sound, networking, and peripheral control circuitry. Each Mac model has a different logic board, but many of the microchips used in different models are the same.

Software and data are stored on a *hard-disk drive* for safekeeping when your Mac's power is turned off and for quick access when it's turned on. A *floppy-disk drive* is used to back up data to 3.5-inch disks and to transfer data between the hard-disk drive and other Macs or PCs. Users communicate with the Mac hardware via the keyboard and mouse, which are used to tell the Mac what to do, and via the video display and speakers, which the Mac uses to tell you what it is doing.

Augmenting this basic set of hardware are special parts that differentiate the models from one another, tailoring the various Macs for different types of users. PowerBooks have battery packs for use during travel, high-end Quadras have extra-large power supplies for use as network servers, and Classics have built-in video tubes for low cost and portability.

Every Mac, whether a classic box or modular "pizza box," a laptop or desktop, new or discontinued, can be grouped into one of four distinct model lines: the classic-style Macs, the midrange modular Macs, the high-end Quadras, and the PowerBook laptops. Regardless of their shape, Macs in all these lines can run the same software and have a high degree of hardware compatibility with each other as well. We'll start our tour of the inside of a Mac with the model line most resembling the original 128K Mac—the classic-style Macs.

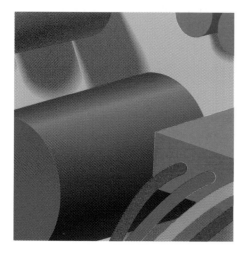

Inside the Mac Classic

THE MOST RECOGNIZABLE Macintoshes are the classic-style Macs, a line that started with the original Mac (known today as the 128K Mac). Perhaps the most popular of all the Macintosh lines, classic-style Macs include the old Mac Plus, SE, and SE/30, and the more recent Mac Classic, Classic II, and Color Classic. Today, the classic-style Mac remains the Volkswagen Beetle of Macintoshes: It won't win any races, but it will get you where you need to go for the least cost.

When first released in 1984, the 128K Mac was a radical departure from the standard personal computer. It had a built-in monitor and small *footprint* (the amount of space a computer takes up on your desk). And, rather than arriving on your desk in the some-assembly-required state of most PCs of the day, the Mac came with everything you needed already assembled inside a $^{3}/_{4}$-cubic-foot case. You could unwrap the Mac from its shipping box, plug it in, and compute. This was part of Apple's original idea for the Mac, to make a computer that could be used by someone who was not a computer expert.

Current classic-style Macs still embody these principles, even more so than the original Mac did. This is because the original Mac did *not* contain everything you needed. It had no internal hard disk, no expansions slots, no video out port, and no more than 128 kilobytes of memory. Today's classic-style Macs have these things and are faster performers as well. And, although it took nine years, Apple finally added a color monitor to a classic-style Mac with the introduction of the Color Classic in 1993.

Few people ever get to see the inside of a classic-style Mac because it is not designed to be opened by the user. In fact, Apple went out of its way to make it difficult to open, using special torx-head screws recessed deep within the case to hold the two halves together, and requiring a special tool called a spreader to open the case. However, to enable users to do their own RAM upgrades, Apple designed the Color Classic with a logic board that slides out the back. There are also no cables to disconnect or reconnect: All connections with the other parts of the Mac are made automatically when the logic board is slid back in. However, even with these improvements in the basic design, the classic Mac is still unique among personal computers in its impenetrable design.

The Mac Classic

Video Display Tube

Instead of a separate enclosed video monitor, the classic-style Macs utilize an internal 9-inch diagonal video tube, which is controlled directly from the analog board. The exposed video tube is the main reason Apple doesn't want users opening a classic-style Mac: The tube is dangerous to you (it can carry exposed high voltages), and you are dangerous to it (it is fragile). Most classic-style Macs display at a resolution of 512 by 342 pixels; the Color Classic displays at 512 by 384 pixels.

Floppy-Disk Drive

A ribbon cable connects the floppy-disk drive to the logic board. The majority of classic-style Macs have a single internal floppy-disk drive. The now-discontinued SE could hold two internal floppy-disk drives.

Hard-Disk Drive

The hard-disk drive stores software applications and data used by the CPU. Internal hard-disk drives communicate with the logic board via the SCSI bus, as do external hard-disk drives.

ROM

The read-only memory contains permanent code used by software applications.

RAM Card

Although the Classic and Classic II contain some memory on the logic board, add-on memory sits on a daughterboard, which plugs into the logic board. Memory is added directly to the logic board on the Plus, SE, SE/30, and Color Classic.

MAC FACT Early Macs had the signatures of the key people on the Mac design team embossed on the inside of the casing.

Analog Board
Named so in contrast to the digital nature of
the logic board, the analog board contains
the circuitry for both the power supply and
the video signals. The power supply converts
110-volt AC power from a wall receptacle
and delivers AC and DC power of varying
voltages to all the electronic parts inside the
Mac, as well as to the keyboard and mouse
on the outside. The video circuitry delivers
display signals to the video display tube.

CPU
The brains of the Mac, the CPU does all the
calculations that make your software work.

Logic Board
The logic board contains most of the
Classic's thinking circuitry, including the
CPU, ROM, and RAM, as well as the cir-
cuitry for the communications and
networking ports.

Input/Output Ports
A standard set of ports connect the logic board to the world outside, including the keyboard and mouse (ADB port), external
hard disks (SCSI port), networks and printers (LocalTalk port),
and modems (modem port).

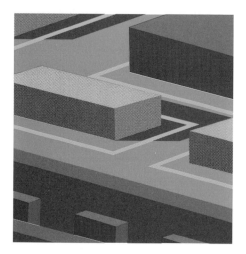

Inside a Modular Mac

THE NEXT STEP up from the classic-style Mac line in processing power and expandability is the modular Mac line, which represents the midrange of Mac computing. The modular Macs come in the more traditional personal computer setup of a box and separate video monitor. Still, they're Macs all the same—designed with much of what you need built-in, but with the assumption that you may want to add more. Modular Macs are expandable, and they are as easy to use on the inside as they are on the outside.

Modular Macs come in many shapes and sizes, represented by three basic lines: the LC, the II, and the Centris, in order of increasing power. The LCs, identified by their pizza-box shape and single expansion slot, represent the low end of the modular Macs. However, not all LCs are the same, with the LC III measuring about twice as fast as the original LC in performance tests.

The Mac II line started with the original modular Mac, the Macintosh II, introduced in 1987. It soon gave way to faster, more compact models with more built-in features. One of the most popular Mac II models was the IIci, the long-time workhorse of mainstream business Mac users. The Centris models represent the high end of the modular Macs and are based on high-performance 68040 processors.

The modular Mac's components are easily accessible to users and can be easily removed. In fact, most modular Macs can be disassembled without removing any screws: The subassemblies are held in place by a system of tabs and slots. Because of this modular design, a nontechnical user can easily swap out a hard disk for a bigger one, as well as add expansion cards from third-party vendors via one of the *NuBus slots*. NuBus is a standard created by Texas Instruments that makes adding boards a "plug and play" operation. There are no switches to set because NuBus cards are self-configuring.

NuBus slots can hold a variety of boards, such as CPU accelerators, network interface cards, and video cards for big, high-color-resolution monitors, which may not be supported by the Mac's built-in video circuitry. And unlike the classics, modular Macs have always been able to run color monitors.

The Modular Mac IIci

Power-Supply Assembly
The power supply is enclosed in a shielded case to reduce electromagnetic emissions and to protect both users and components. Like the other components of a modular Mac, the power supply pops out for easy replacement. The assembly snaps into a connector, which delivers power to the logic board; power flows from the logic board to all internal components, as well as to the NuBus slots and external ports. A cable from the external monitor to the back of the power assembly supplies the monitor with power.

NuBus Slots
These slots hold expansion boards that communicate with the logic board, which recognizes all the cards in the NuBus slots. The number of NuBus slots varies from one to six, depending on the Mac model.

Logic Board
As in the classic-style Macs, the logic board in the modular Macs contains the CPU, RAM, and all other digital circuitry. The logic board of the IIci and later modular Macs also contains video circuitry to drive an external monitor, thus freeing up a NuBus slot for other add-in boards. The video circuits lead to an external connector that accepts a cable from the monitor.

MAC FACT Built-in CD-ROM drives—devices that play read-only optical discs and audio CDs—made their Mac debut in the Mac IIvx (also packaged as the Performa 600) in 1992. Apple also offered built-in CD-ROM drives with the newer Centris Macs.

CPU

Although the Motorola 68020 chip was used in the original Mac II, the IIci uses the more powerful 68030 chip. The Centris line uses the still more advanced 68040 CPU.

Hard-Disk Assembly

In most modular Macs, the hard-disk drive is bolted to an assembly bracket, which then snaps into place in the Mac. A ribbon cable connects the internal hard-disk drive to the SCSI bus circuitry of the logic board, which is also connected to any external hard-disk drives.

Floppy-Disk Assembly

A ribbon cable connects the floppy-disk drive to the logic board, but the connection does not use SCSI. Instead, it uses a custom controller chip called the IWM, short for Integrated Woz Machine, named after its inventor, Apple cofounder Steve Wozniak.

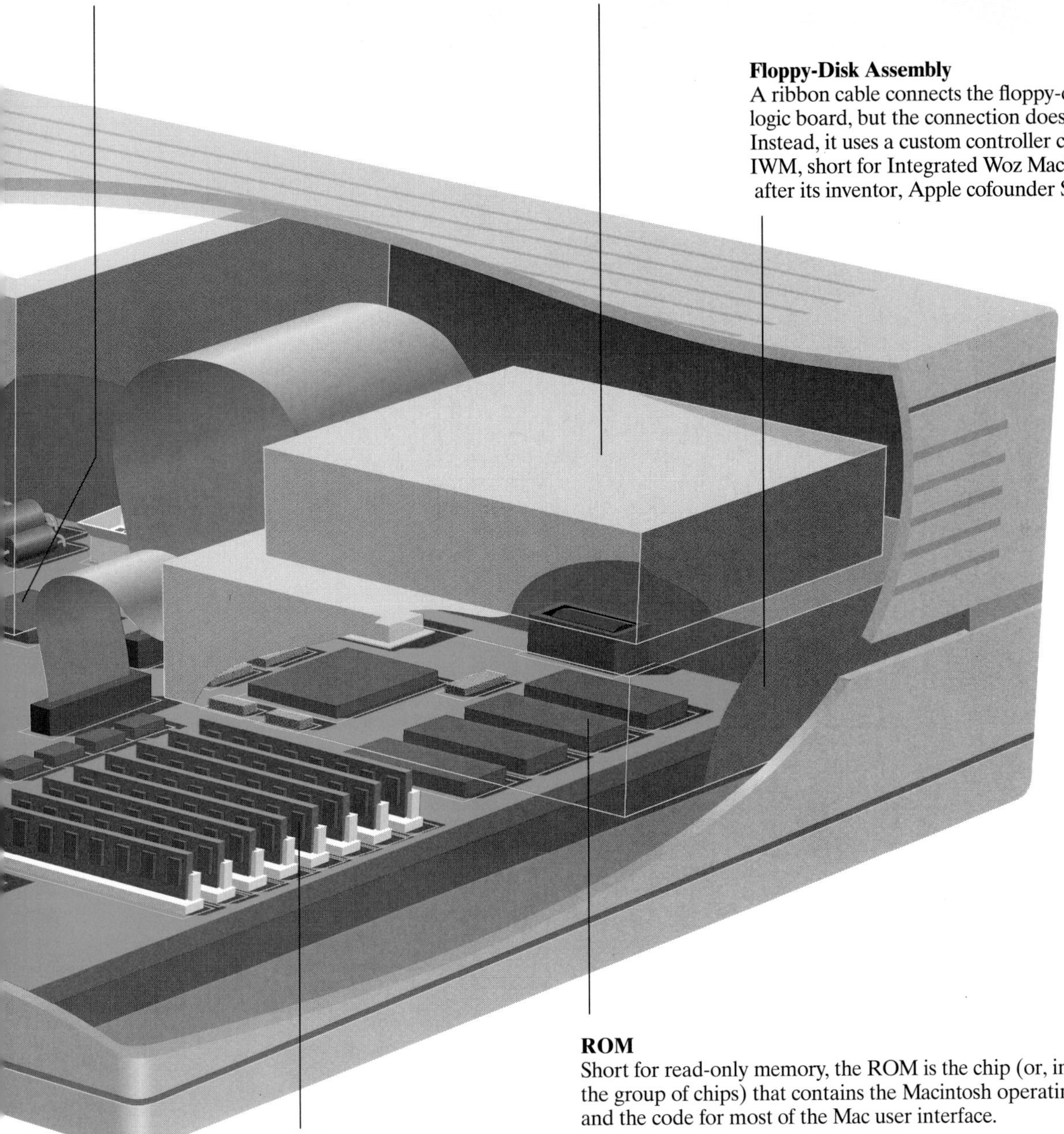

ROM

Short for read-only memory, the ROM is the chip (or, in this case, the group of chips) that contains the Macintosh operating system and the code for most of the Mac user interface.

RAM

Memory in the modular Macs is user installable, a simple matter of snapping RAM SIMMs (single in-line memory modules) into place.

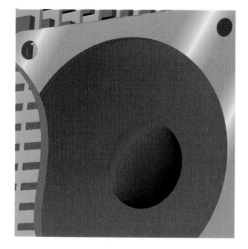

Inside the Quadra

THE MOST POWERFUL 680*x*0-based Macs, the Quadras are designed to fill the role of a high-end workstation or network file server. Built for high performance and with lots of room for expansion, Quadras are used for professional desktop publishing, for graphical illustration (such as the illustrations in this book), and in applications that require tough number crunching and large amounts of storage.

Quadras include the discontinued 700 and 900 models and the more recent 800 and 950 models. Although the Quadra 700 is the same size as a IIci, the Quadra 900 and 950 are not desktop machines at all, but come in a tower configuration, which stands upright next to or under a desk. The Quadra 800 comes in a smaller, mini-tower configuration.

In addition to using the fastest 68040 CPUs available, each Quadra model features faster and bigger components than other Macs. Quadras can hold more memory and internal storage devices, and they can deliver higher resolution video, including 32-bit video (for over 16 million colors) built onto the logic board. Quadras also have enhanced input/output circuitry for faster access to the serial and SCSI ports. And in addition to the LocalTalk network interface built into every Mac, Quadras include an Ethernet port for connecting to high-speed local area networks.

Of course, computer technology is constantly evolving, and Quadras won't be the last word in high-end Mac processing. Already in the works is Apple's PowerPC-based unit, the first Mac-compatible computer to use a RISC CPU instead of a 680*x*0 processor. RISC (reduced instruction set computing) chips are faster than the CPUs in today's Macs and PCs, which means that the PowerPC-based computer will eventually take over as the top Mac.

Quadra 950

Keyed On/Off Switch
This removable key prevents users from accidentally turning the Quadra off; it also prevents unauthorized people from turning the Quadra on.

Power Supply
This 303-watt power supply is the largest in a Mac so far. It provides enough power to run storage devices in all the storage bays, as well as five expansion cards in the NuBus slots and one card in the processor direct slot (PDS).

PDS
The processor direct slot (PDS) in the Quadra is a general-purpose, high-speed expansion slot with a direct line to the CPU, similar to the expansion slot in some other Mac models. A Mac can have only a single PDS. Both the PDS and the NuBus slots can be used at the same time.

RAM
Using SIMMs that contain 16 megabytes each, the Quadra 950 can hold up to 256 megabytes of memory, over two-thousand times the amount of RAM in the original Mac.

4-inch Speaker
All Macs since the 128K Mac have been able to play sounds, but this large speaker makes the Quadra one of the best-sounding Macs ever. A custom sound chip drives a stereo sound output port for connection to headphones or speakers.

MAC FACT On average, the Quadra 950 is 3 times faster than the IIci, 6 times faster than the LC II, and over 12 times faster than the Classic.

Storage Bays
Although other Macs can hold a single internal hard-disk drive, Quadras can hold four storage devices. The front bay can hold a CD-ROM or erasable magneto-optical drive.

Built-in Ethernet
The logic board contains both the LocalTalk and the faster Ethernet network interfaces, making the Quadra a flexible choice for a file server.

NuBus Slots
The Quadra 950 has five NuBus expansion slots, which can run the same expansion cards as the NuBus slots in modular Macs. With video and Ethernet already on the logic board, you have a full five free slots for other purposes.

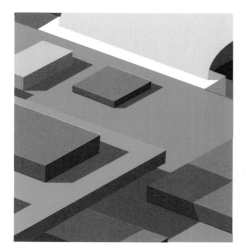

CHAPTER
4

Inside the PowerBook

THE POWERBOOK SERIES, the most radical redesign of the Macintosh to date, was also a radical redesign of the laptop computer. The keyboard sits back toward the display screen, providing room to maneuver your arms in tight places as well as a comfortable place to rest your wrists while typing. And although trackballs are a clip-on afterthought on many laptop computers, the PowerBook integrates the trackball in an ergonomic and convenient central position. This lets you use the trackball without removing your hands from the keyboard. Also radical for a laptop computer is the ability to easily connect external devices such as mice, keyboards, hard disks, and in some models, monitors.

There are two types of PowerBooks: the original line and the lighter-weight PowerBook Duos. The original PowerBook has the same external ports as a desktop Mac, including a SCSI port, printer and modem ports, an Apple Desktop Bus (ADB) port for external keyboard and mouse, and in some cases, a port for standard color video monitors. There is also an AC power plug and battery for power and a slot for an internal modem.

The Duo is both a laptop and desktop Mac, splitting the Mac functions into two parts. The 68030 CPU, RAM, hard disk, and a serial port are in the laptop, while a desktop docking station called the Duo Dock contains room for another hard drive, a floppy drive, most of the input/output circuitry, and ports, including SCSI and video output. This lightens the weight of the laptop component of the Duo system to a mere 4 pounds (compared to 7 pounds for the original PowerBook), with a thickness of less than $1^1/_2$ inches. The Duos also contain a nickel-hydride battery, which provides longer life than the nickel-cadmium (NiCad) batteries of the original PowerBook.

When docked, a Duo has everything that a desktop Mac has and more than a standard PowerBook, including two NuBus expansion slots, which are built into the Duo Dock. There are also lighter, more compact docks available from Apple and third-party manufacturers; they take the form of light-weight bars that you plug into the back of the Duo. These docking bars let you take some of the ports normally available only when the Duo is docked on the road with you, and they can provide special features such as Ethernet ports or support for large monitors.

Like the classic-style Macs, PowerBooks are not user serviceable, because of the fragile components inside. Also like classic-style Macs, all PowerBooks have built-in displays, but in the PowerBooks they are low-power, flat-panel displays. PowerBook displays come in monochrome, gray-scale, and color versions, but color displays draw more power and shorten battery life. All PowerBooks come with power-saving software, which turns off the display and hard-disk drive after a set period of inactivity.

PowerBook 180

▢ MAC
FACT Apple's first attempt at a battery-powered Mac, the Macintosh Portable, had a battery life of almost 12 hours, but weighed in at 17 pounds. It wasn't what users wanted, and Apple sold less than 100,000 units. The 7-pound PowerBook, with a 3-hour battery life, was an instant success and became the best-selling laptop computer ever: Apple sold $1 billion worth during the product's first year alone.

Display
All PowerBooks (including the Duos) come with one of two types of display: liquid crystal display, also called passive matrix, or active matrix. The latter provides sharper images, but is more expensive. Both are lit from behind with low-power lamps.

Built-in Microphone
This can be used to record your own system beeps or take vocal notes.

Floppy-disk drive
This drive is completely compatible with desktop models, though it is smaller and lighter.

RAM Card
Although 4MB of RAM sits on the logic board, new RAM can be added via a circuit board called a daughterboard. Unlike desktop Macs, PowerBooks do not use SIMMs.

Logic Board
PowerBooks have the smallest and lightest logic board of the Macs. Connections to the hard disk are made with a flexible circuit board, which is lighter, but much more fragile, than a wire cable.

Battery
Most PowerBooks use a rechargeable NiCad battery, which can be recharged while in use. The battery slides out the left side for easy replacement. System software can greatly increase battery life by occasionally putting the PowerBook in sleep mode, which slows the processor clock speed and turns off the hard disk and screen back-lighting after set periods of inactivity.

Modem Card
The internal modem slot accepts a modem less than 2 inches long. Most internal PowerBook modems run at 9,600 or 14,400 bps and have fax capabilities.

Trackball
Basically an upside-down mouse, the ball turns two wheels, which relay the left/right and up/down movements of the ball to the logic board. The logic board uses this information to control the position of the arrow cursor on screen. The wheels are also sensitive to the speed of the ball's motion: A slow movement of the ball moves the cursor a small distance on screen, and a rapid movement of the ball moves the cursor a greater distance.

Hard-disk drive
Hard drives in PowerBooks usually weigh 6 ounces or less and contain disks 2.5 inches in diameter.

PowerBook Duo 230 and Duo Dock Docking Station

NuBus Slots
Two NuBus slots in the Duo Dock can accept the standard expansion cards used in desktop Macs.

1 The power latch pulls the closed PowerBook Duo into the Duo Dock like a VCR sucking in a video tape. While this happens, the PDS connectors on the PowerBook Duo and the Duo Dock are plugged together. The power latch also ejects the PowerBook Duo. In the desktop configuration, an external keyboard and monitor are used with the PowerBook Duo's internal CPU and memory.

2 The expansion connector is a 152-pin PDS slot connector, which transmits signals from the PowerBook Duo's CPU to the SCSI bus, NuBus, and floppy-disk drive, as well as to the video and other ports on the Duo Dock. The PDS connector on the Duo can also plug into smaller docking bars.

3 The Duo Dock logic board contains the video controller circuitry for an external monitor as well as for the input/output control. There is no CPU or RAM on this logic board; the CPU and RAM in the PowerBook Duo are used.

MAC FACT PowerBook Duos can work nicely as desktop Macs and are as fast as midline desktop Macs. For instance, the PowerBook Duo 230 has proven to be 35 percent faster than the IIci in MacUser Labs performance tests.

Ports
The Duo Dock supplies the standard Mac ports: SCSI, standard video, two serial ports, sound in and out ports, and Apple Desktop Bus ports for an external keyboard and mouse.

Power Supply
The Duo Dock has its own 75-watt power supply to convert AC power from the wall to power for the Dock's components and to charge the PowerBook Duo's battery.

Floppy-disk Drive
The Duo Dock contains a built-in floppy-disk drive and a port for an external floppy-disk drive.

Optional Dock Hard-disk Drive
In addition to the hard-disk drive in the PowerBook Duo, the Duo Dock itself has a storage bay for an optional second hard-disk drive.

THE SYSTEM

C O N T E N T S

OVERVIEW

THE SYSTEM SOFTWARE is what makes the Mac run. It starts up the Mac, displays graphic images on the screen, and communicates with other computers on networks. It creates the windows, menus, dialog boxes, and most every other part of the word processors, spreadsheets, and other programs you run. The system software is what makes the Mac a Mac.

The system is not a single piece of software, but a collection of software routines, some stored in the System Folder on the hard disk, and others stored more permanently in ROM (read-only memory) on the logic board of every Mac. The system software consists of the operating system and the Macintosh Toolbox in ROM, the System file and resource files in the System Folder, and the Finder. When first introduced in 1984, the Mac system software was very different from other operating systems, even the one on the Apple II computer. First, the operating system—the software that controls the computer's hardware—is not a monolithic entity in the Mac, but a modular collection of routines. This modularity enables changes to be made to the operating system years after the original design while maintaining compatibility with older hardware and software.

Another surprising thing about the Mac Operating System is that it is just a small part of the system software. A bigger part is the Macintosh Toolbox, which is a collection of procedures and functions used by the applications you run. The Toolbox is responsible for the Mac interface and is one of the reasons why all Mac programs look and work the same. One of the jobs of the Toolbox is to manage libraries of code, called resources. The resource files in the System Folder contain the standard elements used by all applications, such as fonts, icons, and sounds. Application files also contain resources, such as menu titles and menu items.

Of course, you'll never have to deal with any of this. On a Mac, the user never sees the operating system. When you're not running an application, you deal with the Finder, the software in the System Folder that provides the Mac desktop. However, the Finder is not a part of the operating system—it is actually another application! It's said that once you learn one Mac program, you know how to run any Mac program. This is no coincidence: It's built into the system.

PART TWO

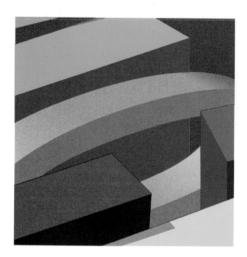

CHAPTER

5

How the Mac ROM Works

THE MACINTOSH ROM contains the most important system software. This tiny integrated circuit chip (sometimes a group of chips, depending on the Mac) contains the Apple proprietary code that defines the look and feel of the Finder and all applications that run on the Mac. And although some of the software found in the System Folder is also required to run the Mac, its main function is to aid, support, and enhance the ROM. The ROM is the heart of the Mac; remove it, and you no longer have a Mac.

The Mac ROM contains libraries of well over a thousand short software routines, each tailored to perform a specific function executed by the Mac's 680x0 CPU. These libraries fit into one of two groups: the Macintosh Toolbox (also called the User Interface Toolbox) and the Macintosh Operating System. Software applications make calls to both the Toolbox and the operating system.

Most of the code in ROM is taken up by the Toolbox, which is responsible for handling the user interface of every application. Toolbox routines are a functional level above those of the operating system, which performs low-level tasks that control the Mac's hardware, ports, and peripherals.

The Toolbox contains a set of common routines that an application can use to create the user interface. This is very different from standard programming techniques for most other operating systems, which require the applications themselves to contain code for the interface. This is why ve.sions of software for Microsoft Windows usually take up more disk and RAM space than the Mac version of the identical program.

Toolbox routines are grouped together into functional sets called *managers*. There are managers for windows, menus, dialog boxes, sound, and others, all of which provide applications with the elements of the Mac interface. For example, QuickDraw, the graphics manager, draws everything that you see on screen—both text and graphics.

People are often surprised to learn that the System file is not the Mac's operating system. Unlike the operating systems on other computers, the Macintosh Operating System is not a single program; it is a collection of routines, like the Toolbox. Operating-system routines are also grouped into manager sets according to function. These managers allocate RAM to applications, control the movement of data to and from hard disks and ports, and enable applications to open, quit, and save files.

Another feature of the Macintosh Operating System is that the user never directly interacts with it—or with input/output and file management—as one does with other operating systems. The Mac has no equivalent to the DOS mode of Microsoft Windows, which enables a user to leave the Windows interface and interact directly with the operating system at the DOS prompt. The Mac user deals only with software applications.

Because all Mac applications use the same Toolbox routines to create their interfaces and the same operating-system routines to communicate with RAM and input/output devices, there is a consistent look and feel among Mac applications. This sharing of interface code also ensures that applications will probably be compatible with past and future versions of system software and Mac hardware. Of course, it is not unheard of for old software to have trouble running on a new Mac model with a new version of the Motorola 680x0 CPU. Upward incompatibility between applications and hardware can occur if programmers don't follow Apple programming guidelines and invent their own code instead of using Toolbox or operating-system routines. However, this occurs in a minority of programs, and it is quite common to find five-year-old software running perfectly well on the newest Mac models.

Although ROM in older Macs often works with brand-new software, the Mac ROM is always being upgraded to include new features with each new version of the Mac. This is why some Macs can run System and Finder version 6, while others require System 7 or later. The reason new software applications can run on old Macs (and therefore old ROM) is that applications don't call Toolbox and operating-system routines by their physical locations inside the ROM. Instead, they use code names that refer to the routines themselves. A table of ROM routine names and locations, which is loaded into RAM at start-up time, directs the application to the specific locations in the particular version of ROM. This backward compatibility has been a part of the Mac ROM since the first Mac.

The Mac ROM

2 The application doesn't have to know exactly where in ROM the procedures are located: The application calls a table, which then directs it to the ROM routines. This way, the ROM in each new model of Macintosh can be different without affecting software compatibility.

1 When the user enacts a command in an application, such as pulling down a menu and selecting the Save command, the application makes calls to the Macintosh Toolbox in ROM, which in turn triggers a chain of procedures.

File   Edit   Arrange
New...
Open...
Close...
Save...
Save As...
Page Setup...
Print...

Window Manager
Event Manager
Menu Manager
QuickDraw
Other Managers
Font Manager
Resource Manager
Toolbox

9 When you quit an application after you save your file, the Process Manager will terminate the application, removing it from RAM. The Process Manager launches an application when a user double-clicks on its icon. It is the job of this manager to share the Mac's CPU among multiple open applications, providing the multitasking environment of System 7 and of MultiFinder in System 6.

8 The Memory Manager allocates and manages the portion of memory used by an application. When an open file is saved, the Memory Manager lets the other managers know where in RAM the file can be found. The memory allocation is constantly changing, depending on what the user is doing within an application.

MAC FACT Mac ROM often contains extra space, which Apple sometimes fills with nonessential data that can be accessed by programmers in the know. Sometimes this material is fun stuff, and other times it is experimental data that Apple is considering for future models. The ROM of the first Mac Classics contained an entire System folder that could be used to start up the Mac without the use of a hard or floppy disk. The key combination that invoked this hidden System folder at startup, ⌘-option-x-o, was disabled after a few months of production.

3 A series of Toolbox sets of routines called managers are enacted. This drawing depicts some of the main managers, but the Toolbox contains many others. The Menu Manager handles how a menu works when the user pulls it down and selects a command. The Window Manager keeps track of multiple windows open on the desktop. The Resource Manager allows the application to read and write system resources, such as the fonts, which reside on the start-up disk.

4 QuickDraw, the Mac's graphics controller, displays the cursor and draws the menu on the screen while erasing the part of the screen behind the menu. QuickDraw is also responsible for drawing the text, graphics, windows, and everything on the screen.

5 Toolbox routines make calls to the operating system, telling it to interact with the Mac hardware. In this example, the Toolbox tells the operating system to save a copy of the file onto the hard disk.

6 The File Manager allows the application to access the file system on the hard disk, where the file is being stored. The Save command replaces an older version of a file with a newer version.

7 In this case, the Device Manager sends data to the hard disk through the SCSI port. It also handles the sending or receiving of data to the Mac's other input/output ports, such as the modem, printer, and ADB ports.

File Manager

Process Manager

Other Managers

Device Manager

Memory Manager

Operating System

ROM

Hard disk

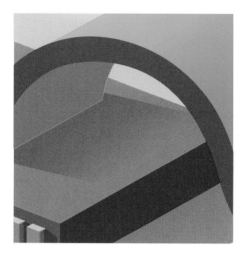

How Startup Works

ONE OF THE busiest times for the Mac is during the first few moments after you turn it on, when there is a flurry of activity that involves most of the Mac's components. It is during startup that the Mac creates the software structures and procedures of its functioning universe.

The creation of the Mac's universe during startup begins with a sort of big bang—a flash of energy that triggers an expanding chain of events. And like the big bang studied by physicists, a lot of the key events that determine the rules by which the system will operate occur in the first few moments. By the time you start to see something happening on screen, the Mac has already checked itself out and established its operating environment.

Because everything in RAM is erased when you turn a Mac off, much of the startup procedure involves loading routines and information into RAM, so that the CPU can access them when needed. The Macintosh Operating System is loaded from the Mac ROM, and the system extensions that add functionality to the operating system are loaded from the System Folder contained on a floppy disk, hard disk, or other type of disk storage device. But before anything can be loaded into RAM, the Mac must find and test its own hardware configuration.

The startup procedure described in this chapter is based on System 7.0 and later. Startup for Macs running System 6 or earlier is similar, except that *system extensions* (called inits in pre-System 7 terminology) and *control panels* (formerly known as cdevs) are at the root of the System Folder instead of in their own subfolders within the System Folder.

Mac Startup Procedure

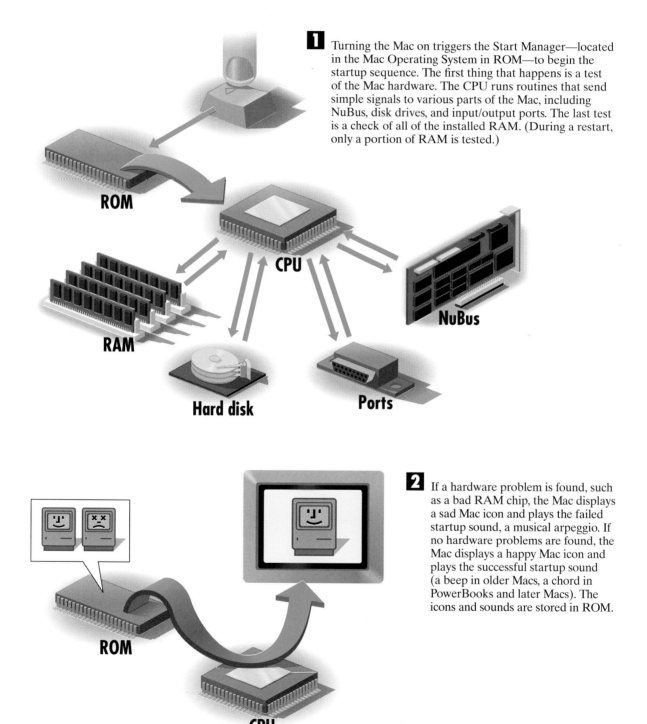

1 Turning the Mac on triggers the Start Manager—located in the Mac Operating System in ROM—to begin the startup sequence. The first thing that happens is a test of the Mac hardware. The CPU runs routines that send simple signals to various parts of the Mac, including NuBus, disk drives, and input/output ports. The last test is a check of all of the installed RAM. (During a restart, only a portion of RAM is tested.)

ROM

CPU

NuBus

RAM

Hard disk

Ports

2 If a hardware problem is found, such as a bad RAM chip, the Mac displays a sad Mac icon and plays the failed startup sound, a musical arpeggio. If no hardware problems are found, the Mac displays a happy Mac icon and plays the successful startup sound (a beep in older Macs, a chord in PowerBooks and later Macs). The icons and sounds are stored in ROM.

ROM

CPU

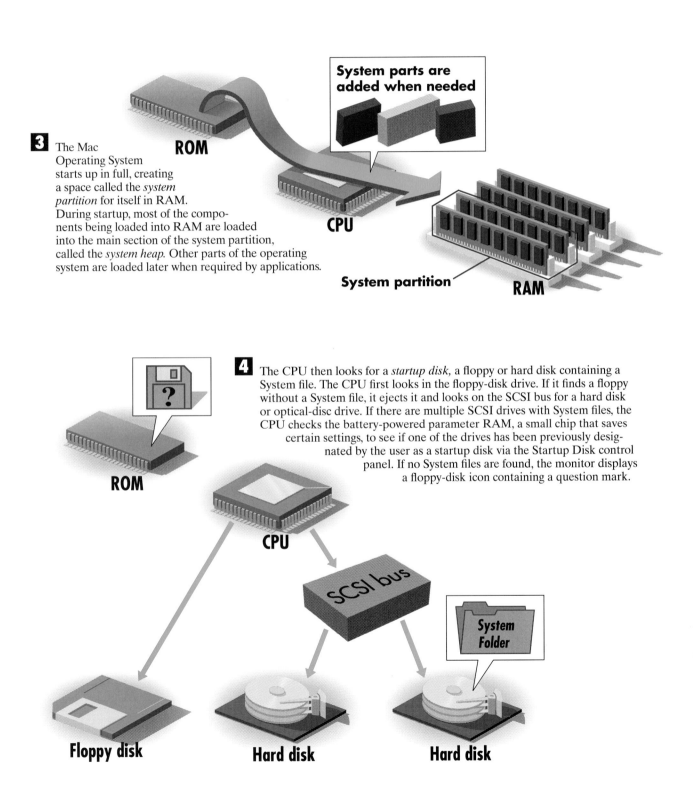

System parts are added when needed

3 The Mac Operating System starts up in full, creating a space called the *system partition* for itself in RAM. During startup, most of the components being loaded into RAM are loaded into the main section of the system partition, called the *system heap*. Other parts of the operating system are loaded later when required by applications.

ROM

CPU

System partition

RAM

4 The CPU then looks for a *startup disk,* a floppy or hard disk containing a System file. The CPU first looks in the floppy-disk drive. If it finds a floppy without a System file, it ejects it and looks on the SCSI bus for a hard disk or optical-disc drive. If there are multiple SCSI drives with System files, the CPU checks the battery-powered parameter RAM, a small chip that saves certain settings, to see if one of the drives has been previously designated by the user as a startup disk via the Startup Disk control panel. If no System files are found, the monitor displays a floppy-disk icon containing a question mark.

ROM

CPU

SCSI bus

System Folder

Floppy disk

Hard disk

Hard disk

Mac Startup Procedure

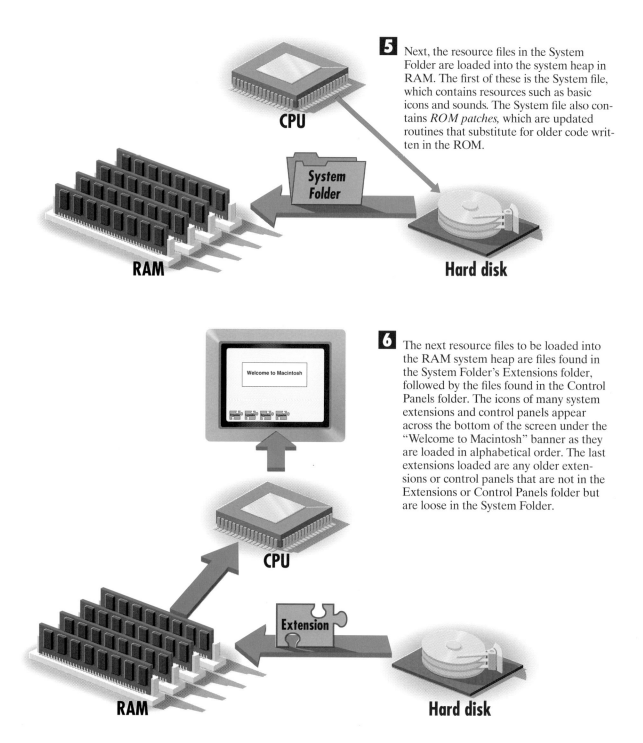

5 Next, the resource files in the System Folder are loaded into the system heap in RAM. The first of these is the System file, which contains resources such as basic icons and sounds. The System file also contains *ROM patches,* which are updated routines that substitute for older code written in the ROM.

CPU

System Folder

RAM

Hard disk

6 The next resource files to be loaded into the RAM system heap are files found in the System Folder's Extensions folder, followed by the files found in the Control Panels folder. The icons of many system extensions and control panels appear across the bottom of the screen under the "Welcome to Macintosh" banner as they are loaded in alphabetical order. The last extensions loaded are any older extensions or control panels that are not in the Extensions or Control Panels folder but are loose in the System Folder.

Welcome to Macintosh

CPU

Extension

RAM

Hard disk

7 The Finder application is loaded into RAM and launched. The Mac desktop, with its icons for disks and the Trash, appears on screen.

8 The CPU looks in the Startup Items folder in RAM for applications (or aliases of applications) and launches them from the hard disk.

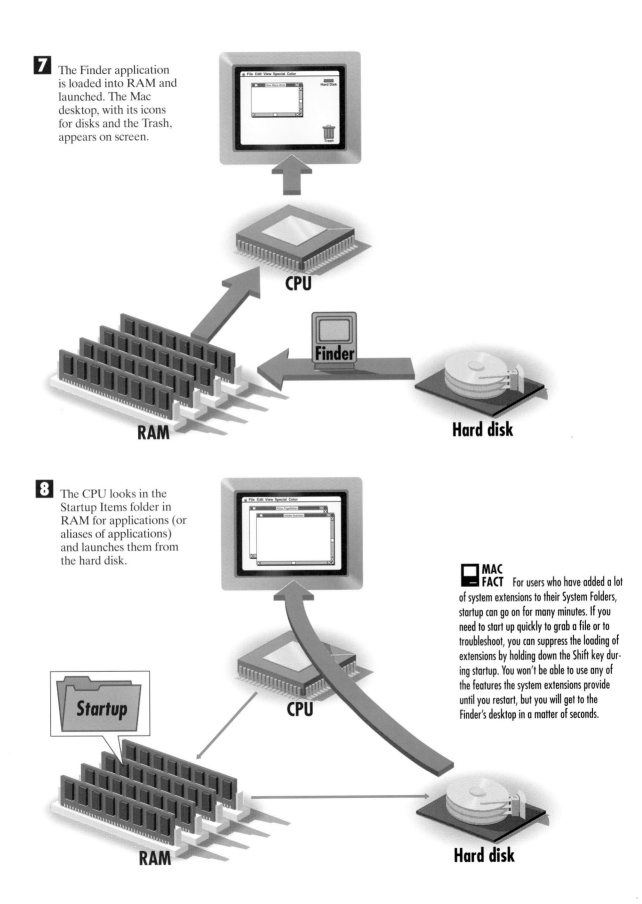

MAC FACT For users who have added a lot of system extensions to their System Folders, startup can go on for many minutes. If you need to start up quickly to grab a file or to troubleshoot, you can suppress the loading of extensions by holding down the Shift key during startup. You won't be able to use any of the features the system extensions provide until you restart, but you will get to the Finder's desktop in a matter of seconds.

CHAPTER 7

How the System Works

ALTHOUGH THE MAC'S ROM supplies the know-how to run software and create the Mac user interface on screen, the System file supplies many of the interface's attributes—called *system resources*. System resources—which include fonts, sounds, menus, dialog boxes, scroll bars, icons, and cursors—are shared by all applications, including the Finder. There are also specific resources in applications, such as menu titles and menu items used by all documents of that application, and in document files, which contain information such as the location of the document window on screen. System, application, and document resources, which are stored on disk, are all managed by the Resource Manager in the Mac Toolbox in ROM.

You can customize your collection of font and sound resources by dropping new ones into the System file. Old ones can be removed by dragging the resources to the trash. However, fonts and sounds are just the tip of the resource iceberg; there are dozens of other types of resources that can be customized, but only with a program such as Apple's ResEdit. You replace many of your Mac's resources every time you upgrade your system or application software.

Although most of the System file's disk and RAM space is taken up by resources, the system also contains routines that augment the code in the Mac Toolbox. Starting with System 7, Apple added Toolbox-like managers that can add features to all applications, but aren't in the ROM Toolbox. Examples include the Program-to-Program Communications Toolbox and the Apple Event Manager, which allows applications to exchange data and to control each other.

In addition to the built-in features of System 7, the system software is designed to allow users to add significant new capabilities by dropping files called *system extensions* into the Extensions folder, which is inside the System Folder. Apple's system extensions offer new classes of functions to all applications without completely rewriting the System file or creating a new ROM chip. Examples of system extensions include QuickTime for the display of video, AppleScript for the automation of data flow between applications, and the Apple Open Collaborative Environment for messaging, directory, and security services. Ordinary extensions (formerly called inits) written by third-party software manufacturers add features to a single program; system extensions are external additions to the Mac Toolbox and enable *any* application to make calls to the new managers. The open design of System 7 allows for the future addition of system extensions not even conceived of today.

The modular nature of the Mac's system software enables the Mac to run with other operating systems while retaining the look and feel of a Macintosh. AU/X, Apple's version of the UNIX operating system, replaces the Mac Operating System at low levels, but enables standard Mac applications to run using the same resources and Toolbox calls they normally do. Programmers can also write UNIX programs that use the familiar Mac interface.

A/UX complies with industry UNIX standards and can run UNIX programs with more traditional user interfaces. These include the Bourne, Korn, and C Shells, which provide command-line interfaces, and the X Window System, a UNIX graphics interface standard. However, A/UX is Mac-like even in the command-line interface, providing point-and-click access to every UNIX file.

Despite its Mac-ness, A/UX is a true multiuser, multitasking operating system, allowing multiple users to connect to one running Mac. A/UX offers many standard UNIX features, including powerful scripting, built-in electronic mail, file transfer, and terminal emulation. A/UX comes with both TCP/IP, the UNIX networking standard, and AppleTalk.

Apple is currently looking at elements of both A/UX and System 7 for the operating system that will run on Macs based on the new high-speed PowerPC RISC (reduced instruction-set computing) processor. PowerPC-based Macs are expected to debut sometime in 1994. The new system software will retain the features of the current System 7, and will make use of resources, Toolbox managers, and an extension architecture.

At the operating system level, the new system software will follow the design of A/UX with a kernel structure called the Microkernel. The main advantage of following the UNIX kernel structure is portability between computers. It is the kernel structure that has allowed UNIX to be easily ported to hundreds of different types of computers, from Macs and PCs to Cray supercomputers. Apple plans to use the Microkernel structure on both PowerPC- and 680x0-based Macs, and possibly on other platforms as well.

The System File and Resources

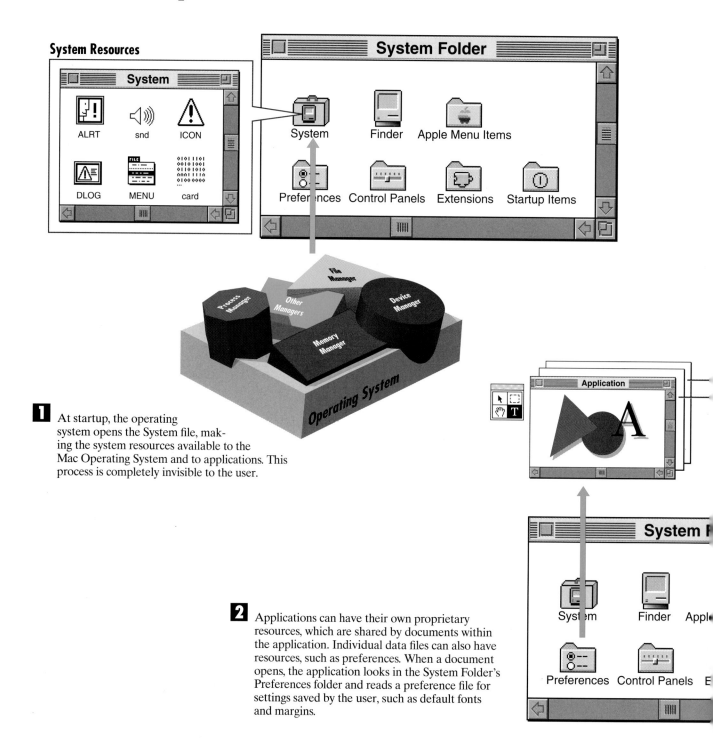

System Resources

System Folder

1 At startup, the operating system opens the System file, making the system resources available to the Mac Operating System and to applications. This process is completely invisible to the user.

2 Applications can have their own proprietary resources, which are shared by documents within the application. Individual data files can also have resources, such as preferences. When a document opens, the application looks in the System Folder's Preferences folder and reads a preference file for settings saved by the user, such as default fonts and margins.

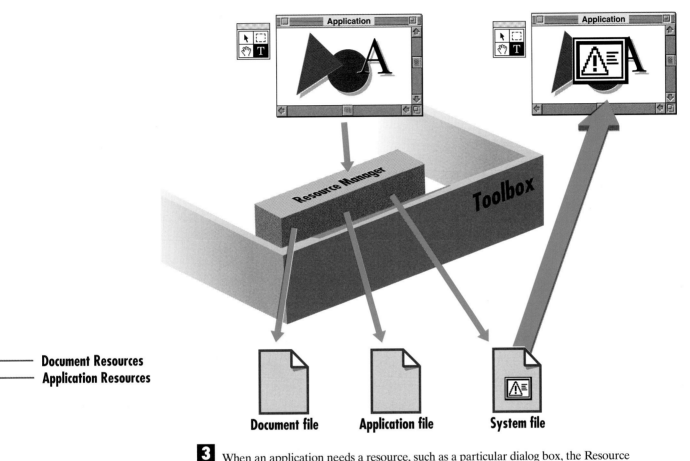

Document Resources
Application Resources

Document file   **Application file**   **System file**

3 When an application needs a resource, such as a particular dialog box, the Resource Manager in the Toolbox typically searches through various resource files. Starting with the most recently opened resource files, it looks first in document files, then in application files, and finally in the System file, stopping any time it finds the requested resource. Applications can also bypass the Resource Manager and specify particular resources for certain uses.

MAC FACT In addition to over a hundred different types of resources contained in the System file, there are lines of code that fix errors (or bugs) in the ROM. These are called *ROM patches*, and they are loaded into RAM at startup. ROM patches intercept calls from applications and the operating system and run the new code instead. Thus, the ROM in old Macs can be upgraded by running new system software.

System 7 Extensions

System extensions—which are the equivalent of new Toolbox routines—can be added to the Mac to provide applications with new classes of functionality. Application programmers can use the new features by adding a few lines of code to their programs to call the new routines. Users add the new functionality by dropping one or more system extension files into the Extensions folder inside the System Folder. The extension architecture is the most important feature of System 7.

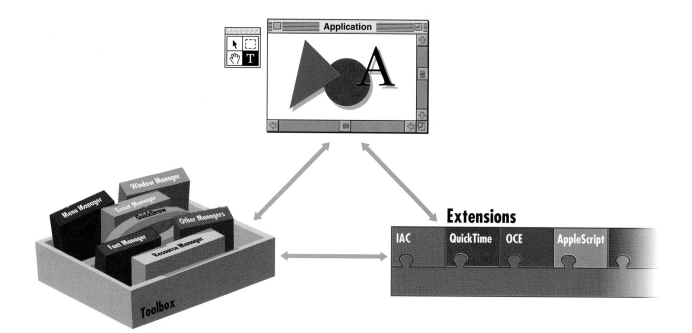

MAC FACT System extensions sometimes follow a migratory path, starting as an add-on extension, then later being included as a built-in part of the system software, and finally becoming an actual Toolbox routine in ROM. 32-bit color QuickDraw, which started out as an extension, was included in the Mac ROM starting with the Mac IIci.

4 QuickDraw displays the video in the application on screen while sound is played through the Mac's speaker. The QuickTime extension ensures that the sound and video are played in sync. If the Mac hardware is too slow to handle the amount of data being displayed, the QuickTime Manager will drop out frames from the video to keep the sound and video synchronized. This is why QuickTime movies sometimes appear jumpy on slower Mac models.

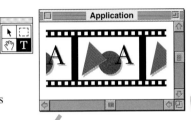

1 One system extension, QuickTime, allows any application that supports QuickTime to display video and sound movies. When a user pastes a QuickTime movie into a file and presses the start button, the application sends a call to the Movie Toolbox.

3 The Movie Toolbox separates the sound from the video. The sound is sent to the Sound Manager in the Mac Toolbox, and the video is sent to the Image Compression Manager, which decompresses the video before sending it to QuickDraw. The Image Compression Manager also compresses a video movie when it is being saved to disk.

2 The Movie Toolbox asks the Mac Operating System to retrieve the compressed movie data—which consists of sound and compressed video—from the hard-disk drive and send it to the QuickTime extension loaded into RAM.

Alternative Operating Systems: A/UX and the PowerPC Microkernel System

Although the CPU can only perform one task at a time, A/UX can run multiple tasks concurrently by scheduling time on the CPU. System related tasks are top priority, followed by tasks that require small amounts of RAM. In addition, the longer a process waits for the CPU, the higher the priority it is assigned. Although the standard Mac system software allows more than one application to be open, it does not schedule which task should be run when. A/UX also allocates each application its own section of memory, which is protected from being overwritten by other tasks.

1 Standard Mac applications under A/UX make calls to the A/UX Toolbox, which accesses the routines in the standard Mac Toolbox. Mac applications can also access system extensions in this manner. UNIX applications with Mac front-ends make calls to both the Toolbox and the UNIX system libraries, which are routines for handling standard UNIX program activities.

2 Standard UNIX programs running under one of the command-line shells make calls to the UNIX system libraries, and don't use the Mac Toolbox at all. The system libraries communicate with the A/UX kernel for file, disk, and memory management tasks.

3 Applications that use the graphic X Window standard are based on the standard UNIX libraries but have an additional layer of code to create the graphical interface. The Mac Toolbox is not used for X Window applications.

4 The core of any UNIX operating system is called the kernel. The A/UX kernel performs some of the tasks of the standard Mac Operating System, such as managing memory and moving data between the CPU and disks and peripheral devices. Mac Operating System routines in ROM are not used when A/UX is installed. The A/UX kernel also keeps track of files, which it treats like much like output devices.

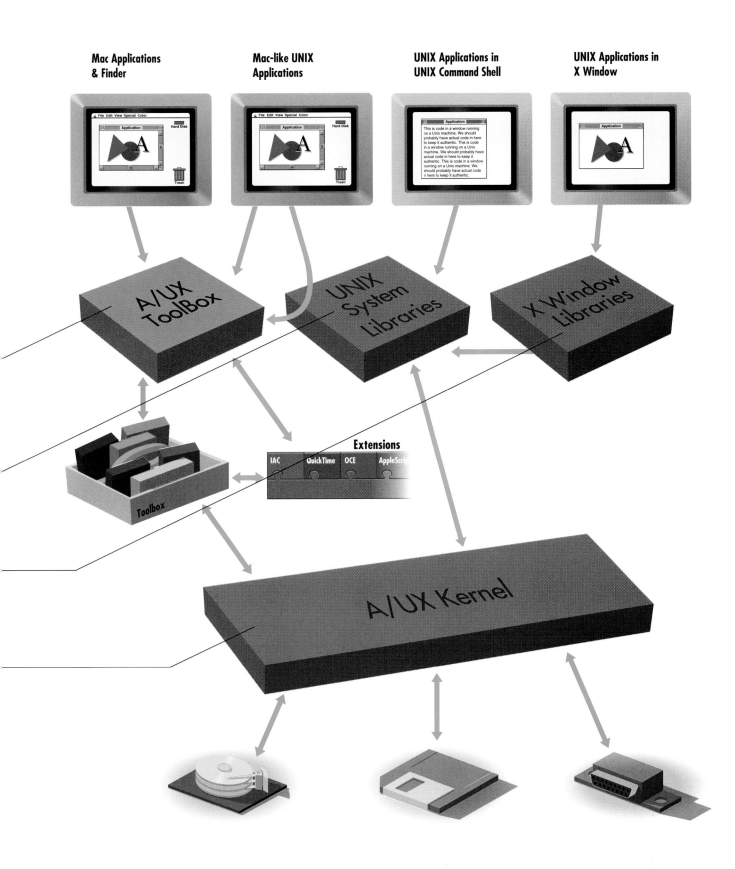

Mac Applications & Finder

Mac-like UNIX Applications

UNIX Applications in UNIX Command Shell

UNIX Applications in X Window

Alternative Operating Systems: A/UX and the PowerPC Microkernel System

Macs based on the new high-speed PowerPC will include new system software to run on the new CPU, which is radically different than the current 680x0 line. The new operating system will have aspects of both System 7 and A/UX.

5 Today's applications will continue to use current Mac Toolbox routines to create their user interfaces, but they will require special software routines to emulate the 680x0 chip. These programs will not take advantage of the speed or special features of the PowerPC CPU.

6 Application developers can choose to port their existing Mac programs to the new CPU through a process called *binary translation*, which will allow applications to run on the new Toolbox routines being developed for the PowerPC. These programs will reap the performance benefits of the new chip, but not some of the new features.

7 Programs written especially for the PowerPC CPU will take advantage of the new chip's speed and features. Because these programs will require the most time to develop, they will most likely be in short supply when the PowerPC-based Macs make their debut.

8 The new operating system will have aspects of both System 7 and A/UX. New Toolbox managers will incorporate the current features of System 7, while the low-level operating system controlling the Mac hardware will be called the Microkernel. Similar in structure to the kernel in A/UX, the Microkernel will provide some of the benefits of UNIX, such as the ability to run several protected-memory applications at the same time.

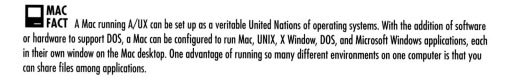

MAC FACT A Mac running A/UX can be set up as a veritable United Nations of operating systems. With the addition of software or hardware to support DOS, a Mac can be configured to run Mac, UNIX, X Window, DOS, and Microsoft Windows applications, each in their own window on the Mac desktop. One advantage of running so many different environments on one computer is that you can share files among applications.

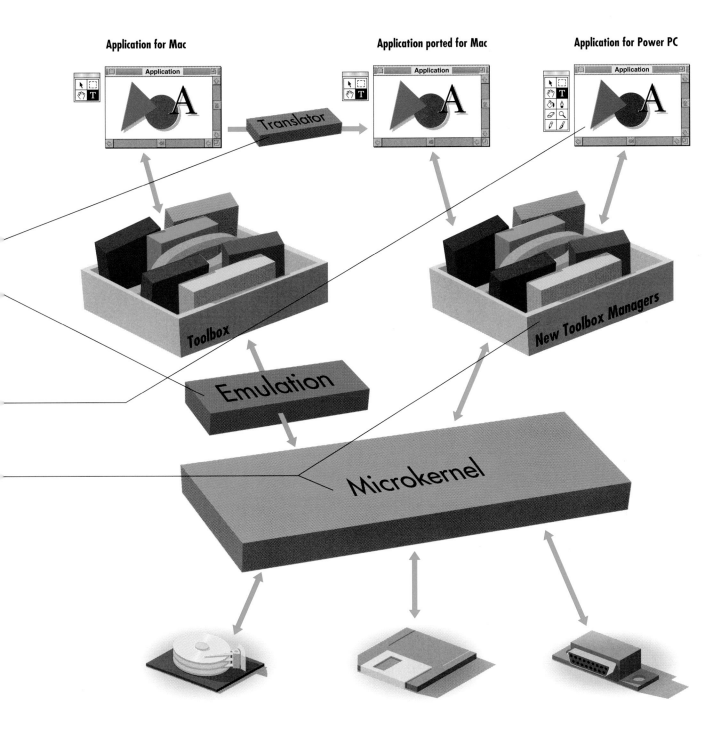

Application for Mac

Application ported for Mac

Application for Power PC

Translator

Toolbox

New Toolbox Managers

Emulation

Microkernel

How the Finder Works

ALTHOUGH IT RESIDES in the System Folder, the Finder is technically not part of the system software. Rather, it is a very specialized application that is launched automatically at startup and from which you cannot quit. The Finder is what Mac users run in lieu of an operating-system mode, which operating systems such as DOS use when no applications are being run. The Finder provides users with the Mac desktop, a view into all the storage devices connected to the Mac. On the desktop, the Finder depicts application and data files as icons or as text lists in windows. It also allows the user to create folders—the equivalent of directories in DOS—to store files or other folders.

The Finder was originally called so by Apple because it locates the files you need on your storage disks. Through the use of an invisible database called the Desktop file, the Finder keeps track of the dozens, hundreds, or thousands of files you may have on floppy disks, hard disks, or other storage devices mounted on the desktop. You also use the Finder to rename and copy files and to delete files by using the Trash.

It is also the Finder's job to *launch* applications—locating the application on a disk, loading it into RAM, and opening the application window on the desktop. To launch a program, you can double-click directly on an application icon or name, or you can double-click on a data file—the Finder can tell which application was used to create a file. The Finder that comes with System 7.0 or later also lets you launch an application by dragging and dropping a file on top of an application. This drag-and-drop method is handy if the file is of a format that can be opened by more than one application.

With the System 7 Finder you can use *aliases* to access files that are buried deep within several nested folders. Aliases are dummy files that are linked to a file. Double-clicking on an alias opens the file it is linked to without having to open any folders.

The Finder also lets you modify your system setup by adding fonts and sounds and changing settings in the control panels. You can even customize your files' icons by pasting new ones into the Finder's Get Info box for each file.

Opening a File in the Finder

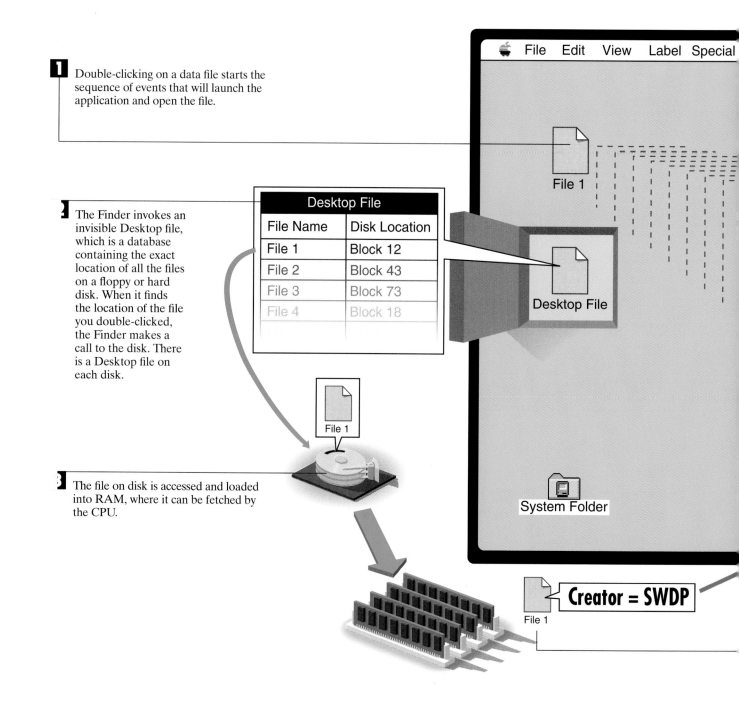

1 Double-clicking on a data file starts the sequence of events that will launch the application and open the file.

2 The Finder invokes an invisible Desktop file, which is a database containing the exact location of all the files on a floppy or hard disk. When it finds the location of the file you double-clicked, the Finder makes a call to the disk. There is a Desktop file on each disk.

3 The file on disk is accessed and loaded into RAM, where it can be fetched by the CPU.

| File | Edit | View | Label | Special |

File 1

Desktop File

System Folder

Desktop File

File Name	Disk Location
File 1	Block 12
File 2	Block 43
File 3	Block 73
File 4	Block 18

File 1

Creator = SWDP

File 1

**■ MAC
■ FACT** Since a disk's Desktop file changes every time you add, delete, copy, or move a file, it can occasionally become cluttered with obsolete information, which slows down Finder performance. It can also become corrupted, which may cause files and folders to intermittently disappear. Fortunately, you can rebuild the Desktop file for each disk by holding down the ⌘ and option keys during startup.

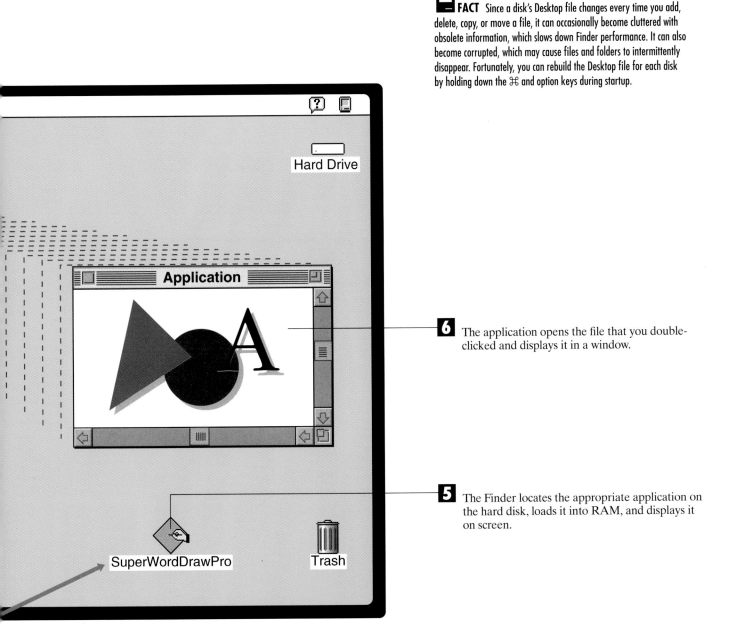

6 The application opens the file that you double-clicked and displays it in a window.

5 The Finder locates the appropriate application on the hard disk, loads it into RAM, and displays it on screen.

4 The Finder reads the file's four-character creator code to determine what application to launch. For instance, the creator code MSWD indicates that the file was created with Microsoft Word. An application called SuperWordDrawPro might have a creator code of SWDP. If there is no application on any disk that matches the creator code, the Finder displays a message saying that the application for this file can't be found.

Creating and Running an Alias

2 After the Finder creates an alias icon, you can move the alias into any folder, including the Apple folder (making it appear in the Apple menu), or you can copy it to another disk. The default name of the alias is the original file's name followed by the word "alias," but you can rename the file to anything you want. You can tell a file is an alias because the characters in the name are always italicized.

1 You create an alias by selecting a file, pulling down the Finder's File menu, and selecting Make Alias.

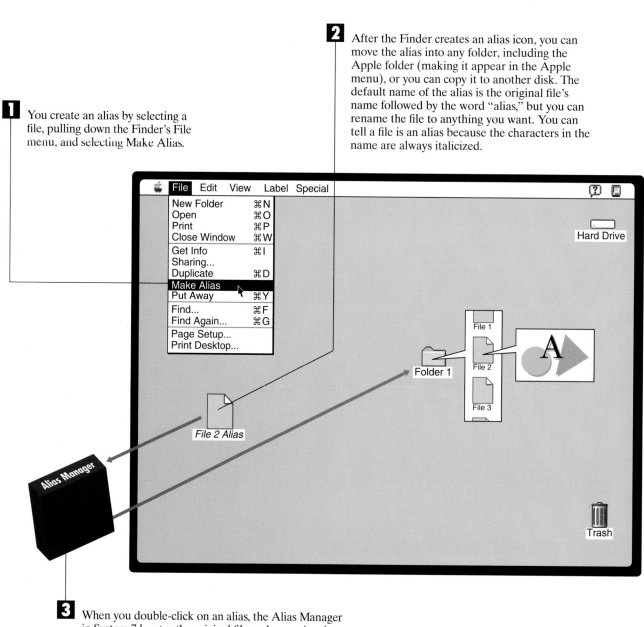

3 When you double-click on an alias, the Alias Manager in System 7 locates the original file and opens it using the normal Finder process (see "Opening a File in the Finder"). The original file will open even if it is buried deep within several folders.

Deleting a File

1 To delete any type of file, you drag the file to the Trash, which is actually a folder. At this point, the file is still completely intact, but it is designated to be discarded. If an application calls for a file that happens to be in the Trash, the Finder sends a screen message asking you to remove it from the Trash. You can drag a file out of the Trash at any time before you invoke the Empty Trash command.

2 When you select Empty Trash from the Special menu, the Finder deletes the file's entry from the Desktop file, and the file's icon disappears from the Trash. Although the Finder can no longer locate the file, it still exists on the disk and can be recovered with file recovery software. However, the file is no longer protected from being overwritten, and it may be partially or totally erased from the disk the next time you save a file.

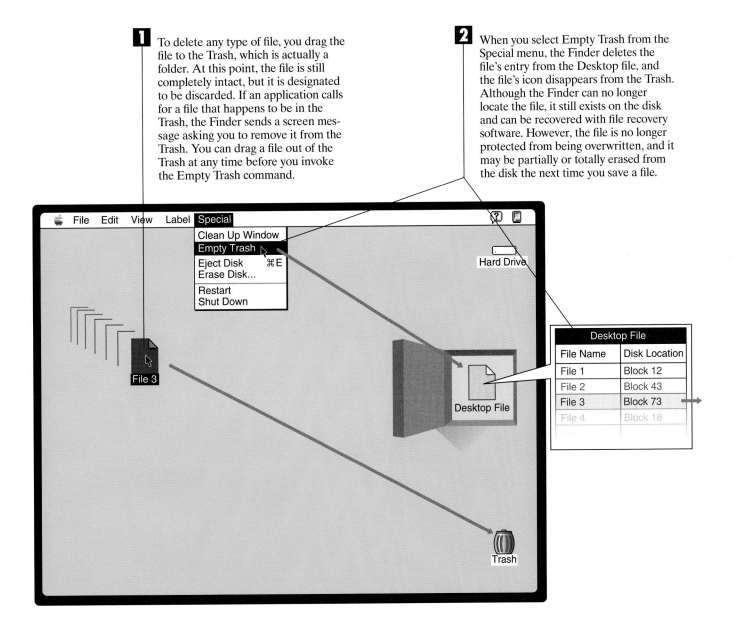

File	Edit	View	Label	Special

Clean Up Window
Empty Trash
Eject Disk   ⌘E
Erase Disk...
Restart
Shut Down

Hard Drive

File 3

Desktop File

Desktop File	
File Name	Disk Location
File 1	Block 12
File 2	Block 43
File 3	Block 73
File 4	Block 18

Trash

MAC FACT Although System 7 and MultiFinder in System 6 both allow multiple application windows to be open at the same time, this was not always the case. Prior to MultiFinder, you had to quit an application before you could go to the Finder or to another application. The first attempt at letting you open multiple applications was a program called the Switcher, but it could only display one application at a time. To switch from one application to another, you pressed an arrow, and the current application slid off the side of the screen while the new application slid in to replace it.

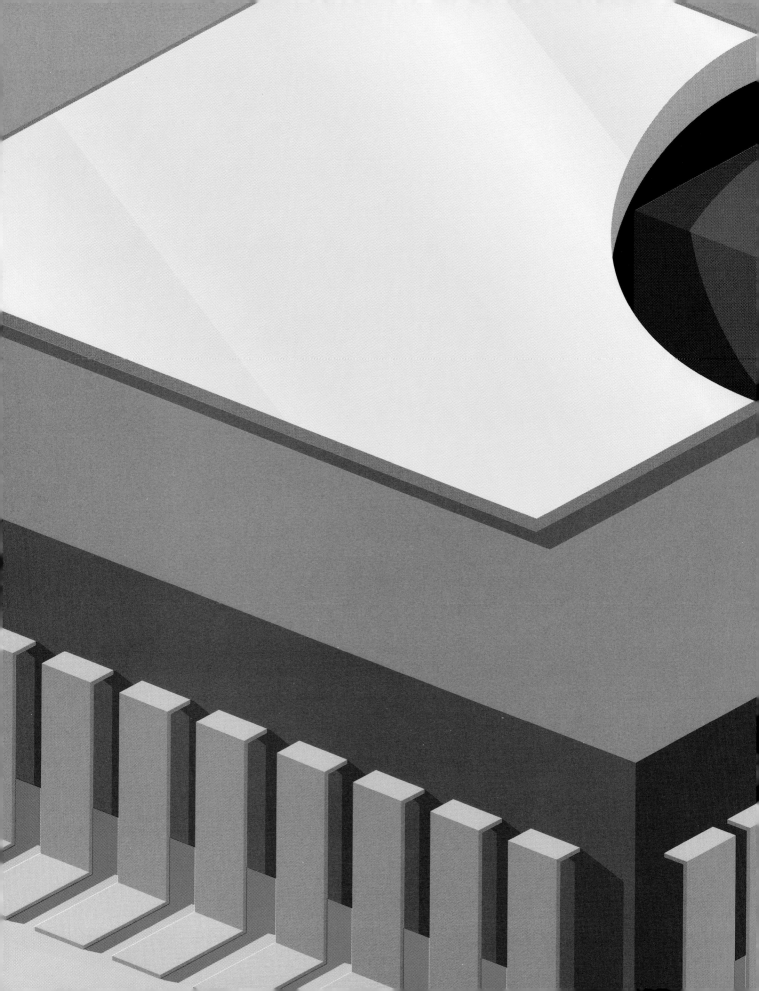

CPU AND MEMORY

CONTENTS

THE CENTRAL PROCESSING UNIT (CPU) and the main memory, also called random-access memory (RAM), are undoubtedly the most hard-working electronic components in a computer. Both are made of tiny silicon chips called *integrated circuits*. These chips each contain thousands of microscopic digital circuits, whose size is typically measured in microns (millionths of a meter). The CPU is a single silicon chip; RAM is a collection of at least eight chips—more in most Macs.

Aiding the main memory in Macs are other short-term stores of information called *caches,* which are used to speed the flow of information. There are different types of caches, but all function to keep the CPU from waiting for information. Caching is used on the logic board, inside hard-disk drives, and inside the CPU itself. The Mac can also perform some other memory tricks, such as using RAM as a virtual storage disk and using a storage disk as RAM (called virtual memory).

The CPU—which on a Mac is one of the chips in the Motorola MC68000 family— is the foreman of the logic board. It calls the shots by making the requests for data and instructions and by processing data. The CPU gets most of its information from RAM, which temporarily stores information loaded from disk-based mass storage devices.

With the CPU executing millions of instructions every second in the form of algorithms and the RAM constantly feeding it data, the operation of integrated circuits can be quite complex. Yet, at its most basic level, the CPU can only count to 1. This is because everything you do with a Mac—from calculating a spreadsheet to drawing a picture to using the Finder to locate a file—is represented inside the integrated circuits as a series of 0s and 1s, or *binary numbers*. The CPU adds and subtracts binary numbers at dizzying speeds, and the RAM stores data in binary form. In addition to pure math, the CPU performs algorithms that eventually translate into actions like opening a window or typing text. This is done by *coding*, designating meanings to certain combinations of 0s and 1s.

Software is called *code* because programmers don't program in binary, but in high-level programming languages that use the letters of the alphabet and English words. When you unravel the code that represents a programming routine to its simplest level, you are left with a string of 0s and 1s.

Binary numbers are used in computers because they are easy to represent electronically. To represent any number takes only two electronic states: high and low voltage (on and off). The 0s and 1s in integrated circuits are represented by transistors, which act as tiny electronic switches. Transistors make up the majority of components in both the CPU and RAM. Resistors and diodes also play a role in digital circuitry, but to a much lesser degree. Cheap, reliable, low-powered, and microscopic in size, the semiconductor transistor is certainly the single most important electronic device today. You can find it in everything from TVs to telephones, from stereos to space shuttles.

CHAPTER

Binary Numbers and Transistors

COMPUTERS USE THE binary number system to count. To understand why we would want to count with binary numbers, let's look at some of the ways we can count. The most primitive method might be to assign a character—a vertical line (|), for instance—to each object we are counting. If we had six sticks, we could represent them as

| | | | | |

The problem with this numbering system is that it becomes unmanageable when the numbers grow large. For instance, 20 sticks would be represented as

| | | | | | | | | | | | | | | | | | | |

To prevent massing a large number of characters, we could assign a unique character to every number. However, we'd soon run out of characters and would have an awful lot to memorize as well.

The decimal system is a compromise between these two systems: It uses ten characters for the first ten numbers (0 through 9) and then uses combinations of these characters to represent larger numbers. We do this by assigning values to places: We have a 1s place, a 10s place, a 100s place, and so on. Each place represents ten times the place to its right; for example, the number 126 tells us we have six 1s, two 10s, and one 100.

In the binary system, we only have two characters—0 and 1—so each place represents twice as much as the place to its right. This gives us a 1s place, a 2s place, a 4s place, an 8s place, and so on. The binary number 1011, then, tells us we have one 1, one 2, no 4s, and one 8. In decimal, that's 1 + 2 + 0 + 8, or 11.

In computer terminology, each binary place is called a *bit,* so 1101 is a 4-bit number. Bits are arranged in groups of 8, called *bytes.* The biggest 8-bit binary number, 11111111, is 255 in decimal (1 + 2 + 4 + 8 + 16 + 32 + 64 + 128), which isn't very big. However, today's Macs can handle numbers that are 4 bytes long, or 32 bits. The biggest 32-bit binary number (32 1s) is the decimal equivalent of 4,294,967,295—enough to add just about any two numbers in one step. However, bytes are used to represent other things besides numbers, such as commands and letters of the alphabet, which are defined by certain strings of 0s and 1s. This is why software is called code.

The reason binary notation is used in computers is that the electronics need only two types of electrical signals in different combinations to represent any number. If computers used the decimal system, they'd need 10 voltages to represent the numbers 0 through 9. The transistor is an ideal device to represent a single binary place, or *bit*. When a polarity is applied, we get a current flow, representing a 1. Reverse the polarity and the current stops—we have a 0.

Transistors are made from the element that gives Silicon Valley its name. Silicon, found naturally as silicon dioxide (aka silica) in quartz, agate, and other minerals, as well as in sand, is an insulator—that is, it won't conduct an electric current. Silicon is turned into a semiconductor—a material that is mildly conductive—when impurities are added. This process is called *doping*. Silicon doped with an element such as phosphorus is called n-type and has a net negative charge. Silicon doped with boron, p-type, has a net positive charge.

A transistor is created by sandwiching one type of silicon between two slices of the opposite type. A metal lead is connected to each of the three layers of silicon, now called the *base, emitter,* and *collector.* In this chapter we'll look at an npn transistor, the type used in most integrated circuits.

The Binary Number System

To demonstrate how binary addition works, we constructed an imaginary binary adding machine. Each place, or bit, consists of a spinning sign with a 0 painted on one side and a 1 painted on the other. Attached to the side of the signs are levers. When the 0 side faces forward, the lever is in the down position. When the 1 side faces forward, the lever sticks straight out to the left, hitting the next sign. The decimal readout on the right displays the decimal equivalent of the binary number.

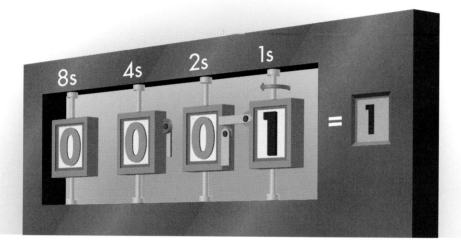

1 We start with 0000 and rotate the sign in the 1s place from 0 to 1. The lever hits the sign on the next column and stops.

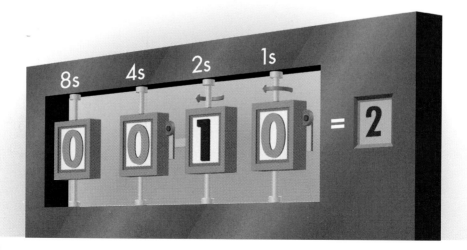

2 To increase the number by 1, we spin the 1s place sign again, returning it to 0. This causes the lever to flip the sign in the 2s place from 0 to 1.

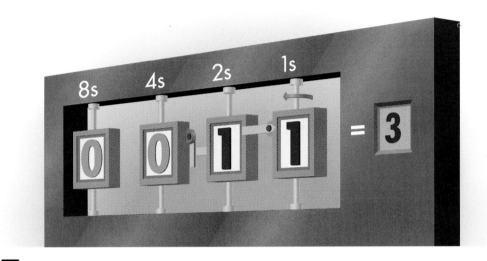

3 Increasing the number by 1 again causes the 1s place to advance from 0 to 1, but doesn't affect the 2s place.

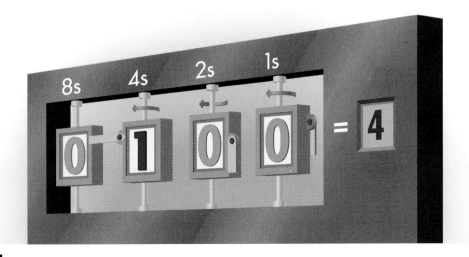

 Adding another 1 to the 1s place causes the signs in both the 2s and 4s places to turn, giving us the binary number 0100, or decimal 4.

A Transistor

A transistor makes use of the fundamental physics principles that opposite charges attract, and that electrons, which are negatively charged, will move from an area of more electrons to an area of fewer electrons. A flow of electrons is a *current*. Applying a small positive charge to the base causes a current to flow through a transistor, putting it in active mode, which can represent the binary numeral 1. By reversing the charge at the base connector to negative, electrons from the emitter are repulsed and no current flows. This case represents a 0.

1 The base of an npn transistor is made of p-type silicon, which normally has a net positive charge. If we apply a further positive charge to the base, we'll draw electrons from the n-type silicon, which normally has a few extra electrons.

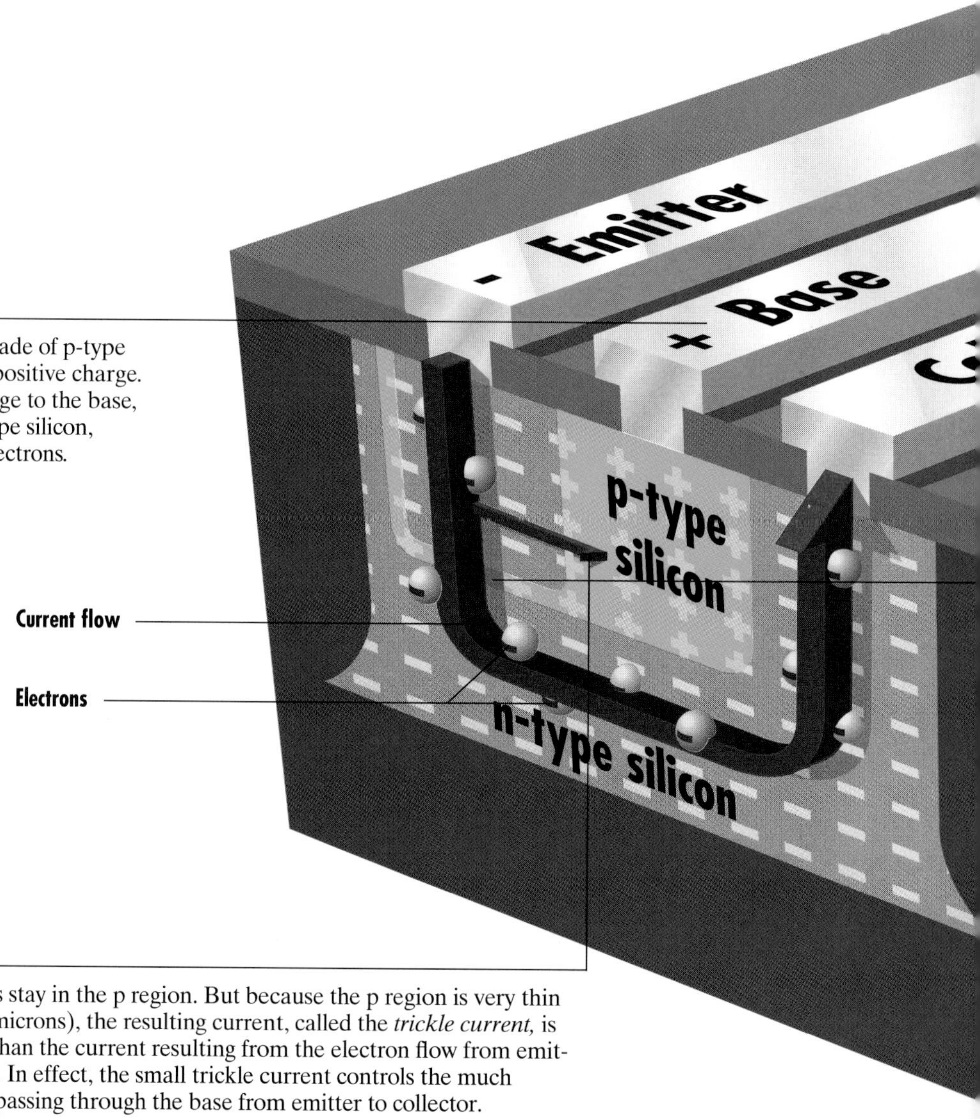

Current flow

Electrons

4 Some electrons stay in the p region. But because the p region is very thin (from .1 to 10 microns), the resulting current, called the *trickle current,* is much smaller than the current resulting from the electron flow from emitter to collector. In effect, the small trickle current controls the much larger current passing through the base from emitter to collector.

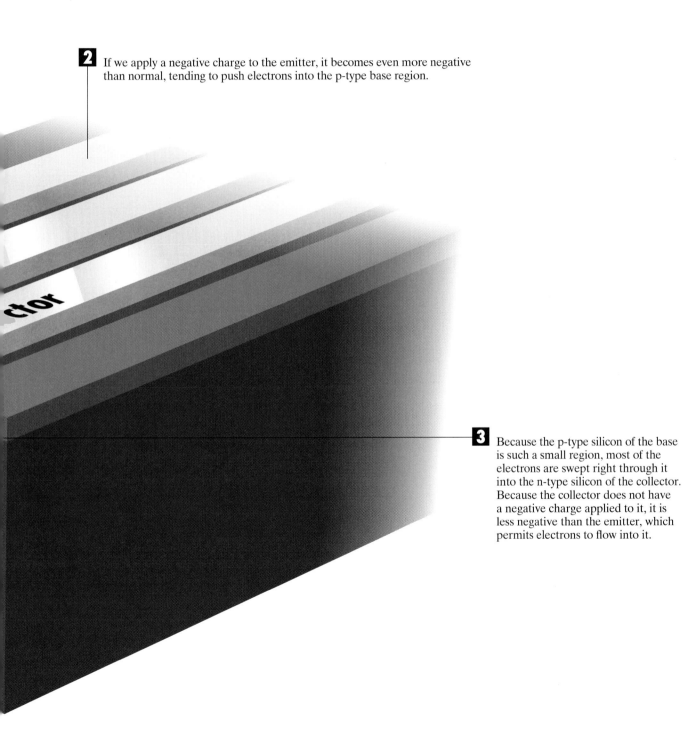

2 If we apply a negative charge to the emitter, it becomes even more negative than normal, tending to push electrons into the p-type base region.

3 Because the p-type silicon of the base is such a small region, most of the electrons are swept right through it into the n-type silicon of the collector. Because the collector does not have a negative charge applied to it, it is less negative than the emitter, which permits electrons to flow into it.

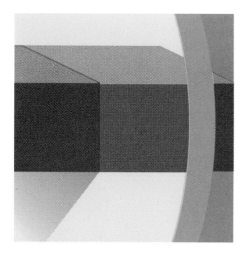

How the CPU Works

ONNECT A FEW transistors together and you have an adding machine. Group a few adding machines together and you have circuits that perform more complex functions. Combine these functions into operational systems and eventually you'd wind up with thousands upon thousands of transistors switching on and off millions of times per second—a microprocessor, a computer's central processing unit (CPU).

The CPU is the brains of a Mac, but it is not a free thinker; it does what it is told to do by software, which consists of the operating system and applications. The CPU accomplishes its assigned tasks by processing two types of information: instructions and data. *Instructions* are commands from the software, and the *data* are the numbers used in the calculations. An instruction is a simple request, and a typical task usually consists of many instructions.

CPUs receive and send information through dozens of pins (the 68040 has 145). These signals are synchronized by a clock, which provides timing signals called cycles, at a constant rate. The speed of the CPU clock is measured in megahertz (MHz), millions of cycles per second. A common misconception is that the higher the MHz rating of a CPU, the faster the computer. Comparing clock speed ratings of different CPUs to judge performance is like comparing the speed of cars by looking only at their engine's RPM ratings. There are other factors to consider, such as whether the CPU processes data in 32-bit or 16-bit chunks, and whether the computer communicates with the CPU in 32-bit or 16-bit chunks. The more bits of information that can be passed around, the faster the performance.

In addition, some CPUs get more done per clock cycle. For instance, the 68000 requires 4 cycles to process an instruction, whereas the 68040 only requires 1.3 cycles on average. The 68040 achieves this rate in part because its design includes several instances of *parallel processing*, which allows certain tasks to be performed simultaneously. The 68040 also integrates a memory management unit (MMU) and a floating-point unit (FPU), which are separate processor chips in other CPUs.

The IBM/Motorola/Apple PowerPC 601, the first of a line of chips to be used in a new generation of Macs, uses RISC (reduced instruction-set computing) architecture. RISC-based CPUs are faster than traditional microprocessors because they use smaller instructions, which can be processed more rapidly. Although more clock cycles are sometimes required to finish certain tasks, clock speeds on RISC CPUs are usually high—the 601's minimum clock speed is 50 megahertz, compared to 25 megahertz in the 68040. Performance is boosted further by the PowerPC's superscalar design, which gives it the ability to execute more than one instruction per cycle. The 601 can execute three instructions per cycle.

The radically different architecture of the PowerPC CPU means that it is not compatible with any previous Mac software, unlike the 68040, which is compatible with software written for 68000-, 68020-, and 68030-based Macs. Current software can run on top of 680x0 emulation software or will have to be rewritten.

Although the PowerPC 601 is several times faster than the 68040, it doesn't include as high a degree of parallel processing as is found in the 68040. This is because the 601 is meant to be the low end of the PowerPC line, with even faster versions, the 604 and 620, coming later.

The 68040 Microprocessor

1 Instructions and data from RAM enter the bus controller, which prioritizes them to keep a steady supply to the execution units, which are the integer and floating-point units.

2 Data and instructions are separated and flow along two separate bus lines, enabling them to be processed simultaneously.

3 New data and instructions routed toward the execution units are copied to the 4K caches, which have 16 times as much cache space as the 68030. The next time the execution units need the same information (which is often in software execution), they fetch it from the caches instead of going to external RAM. The caches also hold intermediate results that require further processing.

4 The memory management units control virtual memory, a System 7 feature that uses disk space as an extension to RAM. The memory management units keep tables of byte addresses to keep track of where the information is.

5 The *integer processing unit* processes most of the information during the operation of the Mac. The 68040's integer unit uses a parallel-processing technique called pipelining to process up to six instructions at a time. Instructions are sent through an assembly line consisting of six stages of execution—a different instruction can be run at each stage of the pipeline. (The 68030 has a three-stage pipeline.)

6 The *FPU* (floating-point unit) can be used for calculations if specified by the software. Floating-point processing is faster for the types of calculations used in financial analysis and in drawing and CAD applications. The FPU in the 68040 has a three-stage pipeline, and can process three math instructions at the same time. Completed calculations are sent back to the bus unit for delivery to RAM.

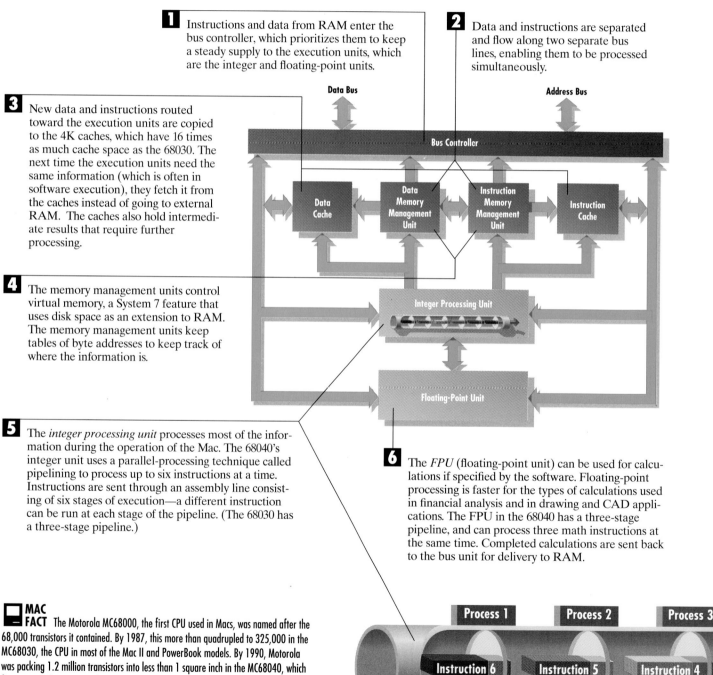

MAC FACT The Motorola MC68000, the first CPU used in Macs, was named after the 68,000 transistors it contained. By 1987, this more than quadrupled to 325,000 in the MC68030, the CPU in most of the Mac II and PowerBook models. By 1990, Motorola was packing 1.2 million transistors into less than 1 square inch in the MC68040, which first appeared in Mac Quadras and Centrises. 1993's PowerPC 601, the CPU for the next generation of Macs, contains 2.8 million transistors in a 1.7-square-inch area.

The PowerPC 601 RISC Microprocessor

1 The bus controller accepts data from RAM 64 bits at a time, but doesn't separate instructions and data into two separate buses. However, the bus unit can pipeline two operations at different stages of bus processing. After prioritizing, information is sent to the memory queue.

2 The memory queue holds the addresses of instructions that are not yet in cache, but are requested by the execution units. When data isn't in the cache, requests go out to the bus. If the bus is busy, the addresses wait in the memory queue until the bus is free. The memory queue also stores new data that has been written into cache and is waiting to be written back to RAM.

3 A cache of 32K (four times that of the 68040) stores instructions and data until the execution units can use them. The 601's cache can supply a large flow of information—256 bits worth—to the execution units.

Data Bus

Address Bus

Bus Controller

Memory Queue

Instruction/Data Cache

Memory Management Unit

Branch Unit

Integer Processing Unit

Floating-Point Unit

Eight-Instruction Queue/Dispatch Unit

4 The instruction dispatch unit is filled with information from the cache in eight-instruction chunks. The instruction dispatch unit feeds instructions to the three execution units as fast as they can take them. The superscalar design enables the dispatch unit to send three instructions at a time, one to each execution unit. The three execution units run independently of each other and can process more than one instruction at a time, so the timing of dispatches can be quite complex.

7 The branch unit is a third execution unit that is used when the computer must skip over to another part of a software program, changing the work flow. The branch unit keeps the branches in the software from interrupting the flow of instructions to the execution units. It does this by looking ahead to see if there are branches and fetching them from the instruction cache in a timely manner.

5 The integer unit of the 601 uses a four-stage pipeline to process four instructions at the same time. Because the 601 is a RISC chip, instructions are smaller, so the integer unit runs at clock speeds above 50 MHz.

6 The floating-point unit, like the floating-point unit in the 68040, does calculations used in graphics-heavy applications. The unit has a 64-bit data path to cache.

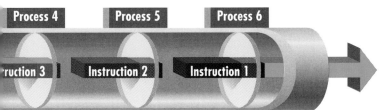

Process 4   Process 5   Process 6

ruction 3   Instruction 2   Instruction 1

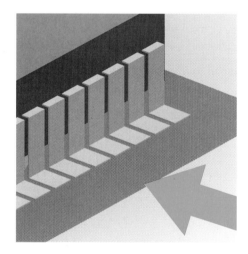

C H A P T E R

11

How RAM Works

THE MAIN MEMORY used in the Mac and most PCs is a type known as dynamic random-access memory (DRAM, or just RAM). It is called *dynamic* because the contents are constantly changing. It is termed *random-access* because the CPU can directly access information stored anywhere inside the chips, just as you can access any part of a phonograph record by dropping the needle down wherever you like on the disk. (A cassette tape, by comparison, is not a random-access medium, because you have to wind through tape in order to get to a section in the middle.)

Most Macintosh memory comes in the form of small add-on cards called single in-line memory modules, better known as *SIMMs*. (PowerBooks, which use their own nonstandard memory cards, don't use SIMMs.) Although SIMMs come in different storage sizes, most contain eight RAM chips, one chip for each bit in an 8-bit electronic word. (There's also a 9-chip version used mostly by government agencies, but it is not common.) Regardless of how many SIMMs your Mac has or how much RAM is soldered on the logic board, all the RAM in a Mac acts as a single pool of memory.

The CPU can access a piece of information stored in RAM by specifying an *address*, a number that identifies the location of each byte of information in RAM. Address 0 and the first several hundred address locations, referred to as *low memory*, are always taken by the system partition, which is created at startup. Applications are loaded into the highest available addresses, referred to as *high memory*.

The memory strategy used by the Mac operating system is called *cooperative multitasking,* in which RAM is dynamically allocated according to the needs of the applications. This strategy enables multiple applications to share the available RAM by running in partitions. The operating system's Memory Manager determines which applications are allocated to which parts of RAM. Usually, only a portion of an application is loaded into a partition at any one time; other parts are loaded as needed.

You can set the size of an application's memory partition by selecting the application's icon in the Finder and choosing Get Info from the Finder's File menu. The suggested size is set by the software manufacturer, but you may want to enter a bigger number if you are working with large files. Up to the point where the entire application is loaded into memory, the bigger the application partition, the fewer times the application will need to go to disk and the faster its performance.

Dynamic Memory in the Mac

2 When an application is launched, the operating system assigns it a partition in high memory. Usually, only a portion of the application and document are loaded into the partition. When additional applications are launched, new partitions are created starting at the highest address and working down. The total amount of memory taken up by an application partition is determined by the memory size setting in the application's Get Info box in the Finder.

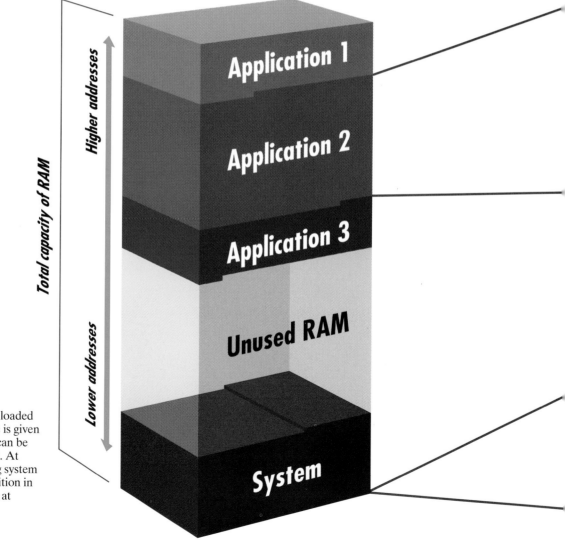

Total capacity of RAM

Higher addresses

Lower addresses

Application 1

Application 2

Application 3

Unused RAM

System

1 When information is loaded into RAM, each byte is given an address so that it can be located when needed. At startup, the operating system creates a system partition in low memory, starting at address 0.

3 Applications call their routines from the application *jump table*, which is a list of an application's routines and their memory addresses. The jump table is stored in the top part of an application partition, known as the A5 World, named after a part of the 68000 CPU called the A5 register. The A5 World also stores application global variables and parameters used by the Mac Toolbox and operating system. The A5 World is static, never changing size while the application is open.

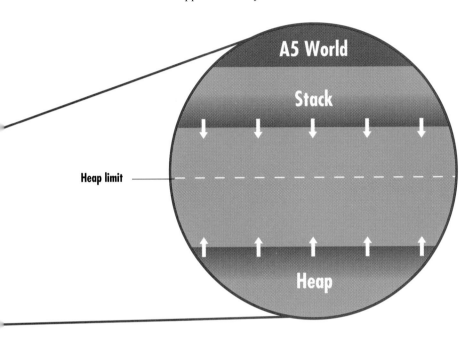

4 Most of the action occurs in the application *stack*, which holds temporary values, and the application *heap*, which holds code segments, resources, and document data. The stack and the heap are dynamically allocated, constantly expanding into and retreating from an empty area of unallocated memory that sits between the two. The application stack can temporarily fill the entire unallocated space, but the heap can fill only a portion of it.

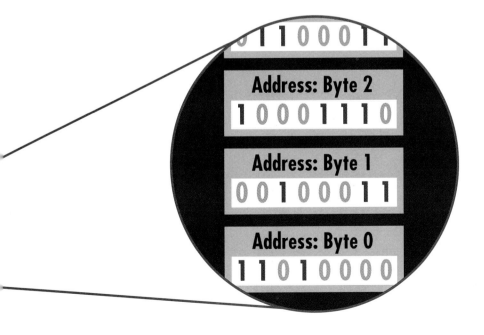

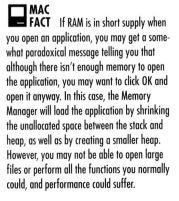

MAC FACT If RAM is in short supply when you open an application, you may get a somewhat paradoxical message telling you that although there isn't enough memory to open the application, you may want to click OK and open it anyway. In this case, the Memory Manager will load the application by shrinking the unallocated space between the stack and heap, as well as by creating a smaller heap. However, you may not be able to open large files or perform all the functions you normally could, and performance could suffer.

Application Stack

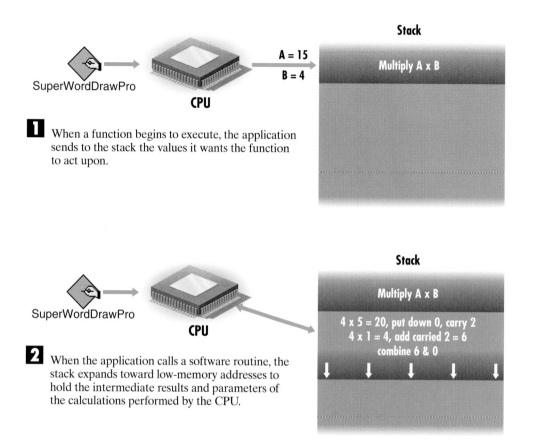

Stack

Multiply A x B

1 When a function begins to execute, the application sends to the stack the values it wants the function to act upon.

Stack

Multiply A x B

4 x 5 = 20, put down 0, carry 2
4 x 1 = 4, add carried 2 = 6
combine 6 & 0

2 When the application calls a software routine, the stack expands toward low-memory addresses to hold the intermediate results and parameters of the calculations performed by the CPU.

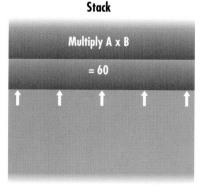

Stack

Multiply A x B

= 60

3 When the execution of the procedure is complete, the stack shrinks to an area a little larger than its starting size. The extra space contains the result of the calculation. The stack area of the application memory partition expands and contracts on a last-in-first-out basis, always remaining contiguous and never becoming fragmented.

Application Heap

1 When an application no longer requires a certain piece of information, such as a routine or piece of data, the Memory Manager releases the space occupied by the information. This is often in the middle of heap.

2 When an application needs a resource, code segment, or data from a file, the information is loaded at the top end of the heap. If the heap grows to the heap limit, the Mac displays a message telling you that there is not enough memory to complete the action.

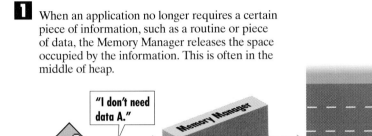

"I don't need data A."

Memory Manager

SuperWordDrawPro

New Data

Data A

3 When multiple areas of free unallocated RAM are formed in the middle of the heap, the memory is said to be *fragmented*. Fragmentation of memory wastes memory space and can prevent an application from performing certain tasks. (A similar condition on hard disks is called disk fragmentation.)

4 When fragmentation reaches a certain level, the Memory Manager *compacts* the heap by moving blocks of information into the empty spaces.

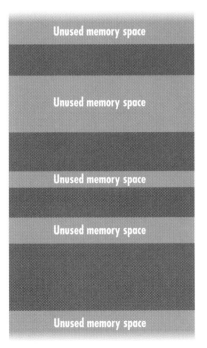

Unused memory space

Unused memory space

Unused memory space

Unused memory space

Unused memory space

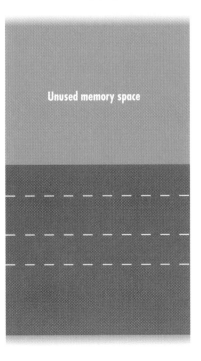

Unused memory space

MAC FACT Most crashes on the Macintosh originate in RAM. Crashes will eliminate information in RAM, but don't harm the Mac hardware or data on the hard disk. If the stack grows into the space used by the heap, the heap can become corrupted, crashing the application. Applications can also crash if you've set the partition size too low. System crashes can occur when two programs think they each control the same segment of memory. Crashes due to competition for RAM don't occur with A/UX, because application partitions are protected from one another.

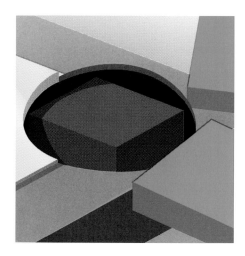

CHAPTER
12

How Virtual Memory Works

EVER NEED TO open just one more application, but find you're 100K short of RAM? This is when *virtual memory* comes in handy. A feature of System 7 and some third-party utilities, virtual memory lets you open more files than you actually have room for in RAM. Virtual memory uses space on a hard disk as an annex to the main memory to store information that hasn't been used recently by the CPU. The CPU treats virtual-memory disk space as RAM.

The amount of virtual memory and the disk it resides on is set in the Memory control panel. Once virtual memory is set up and turned on, the Mac acts as if you had added more SIMMs. In the About This Macintosh window in the Finder, the number displayed for total memory will include the amount of disk space you've reserved for virtual memory.

The drawback to virtual memory is that it is slow; disk access is many hundreds of times slower than RAM access. It is therefore not a good idea to rely too heavily on virtual memory. Optimally, the application you are working on should fit in real RAM, and open applications not being used should be in virtual memory. Virtual memory will run more smoothly when several applications are open, rather than when a single application with one large file is loaded. You should also avoid running background tasks in other applications, which may cause frequent swapping between RAM and the virtual-memory portion of the hard disk and lead to very slow performance.

Whether you're using System 7 or a third-party utility, virtual memory is available in Macs with 68030 or 68040 CPUs, and in 68020-based Macs equipped with a Motorola 68851 memory management unit (MMU, also called a paged MMU, or PMMU). 68030s and 68040s have built-in MMU functions. Older 68000-based Macs, such at the SE, the Classic, and the PowerBook 100, cannot use virtual memory.

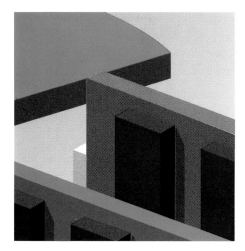

CHAPTER 13

How a Cache Works

WHEREAS VIRTUAL MEMORY (described in the previous chapter) lets you open more applications at the expense of performance, there is a memory trick called caching that helps applications work faster and more efficiently. A *cache* is a temporary storage place that sits between the CPU and a storage medium. Its purpose is to feed the CPU information as fast as it requests it. This means that the CPU doesn't have to wait, and performance is improved.

Caches are used in a lot of places in and around your Mac, such as in the CPU itself (as we saw in Chapter 10), as well as in external storage devices such as hard-disk drives and CD-ROM drives. There are two main types of cache that can be used in the Mac: a RAM cache and a disk cache. As the names imply, a RAM cache speeds up RAM access, and a disk cache speeds up disk access.

A RAM cache is usually added to a Mac in the form of an expansion card. Most Macs can accept a RAM cache card, but the Mac IIci and IIvx each have a slot specially designed for a cache. In fact, for the second half of the IIci's production run, a RAM cache card was added to the Mac as standard equipment. It helps for the cache medium to be faster than the medium from which it is caching, so a RAM cache is often made of high-speed static RAM, which is at least three times faster than the dynamic RAM used in main memory. Static RAM is expensive, but you don't need much— a 32K or 64K RAM cache can boost performance by 30 to 60 percent.

A disk cache uses a piece of the Mac's RAM to temporarily hold information from a disk storage device. As was mentioned in Chapter 12, it is several hundred times faster to access information from dynamic RAM than from a disk, so using a disk cache improves performance. Disk caching is built into the Mac's system software. (System 6 erroneously labeled it a RAM cache, which caused a lot of confusion among users and journalists. Fortunately, Apple corrected this in System 7.) You can set the size of the cache you want to use in the Memory control panel, but you can't shut it off. The optimum disk cache varies with the types of applications you use, but Apple recommends setting 32K of disk cache for every megabyte of RAM installed.

A RAM Cache

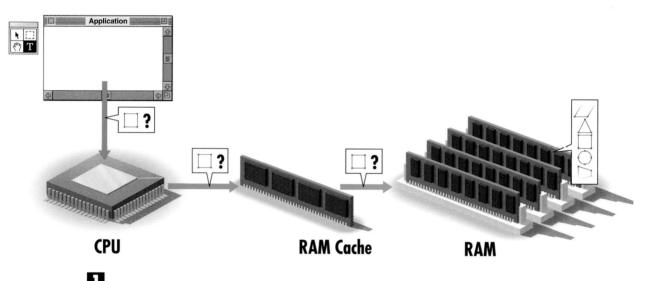

1 When an application requests a piece of information (program code, file data, a resource, or anything else stored in RAM), the CPU sends a query to RAM. The RAM cache intercepts the request and searches itself for the information. If it does not have the requested information, it passes the query along to RAM.

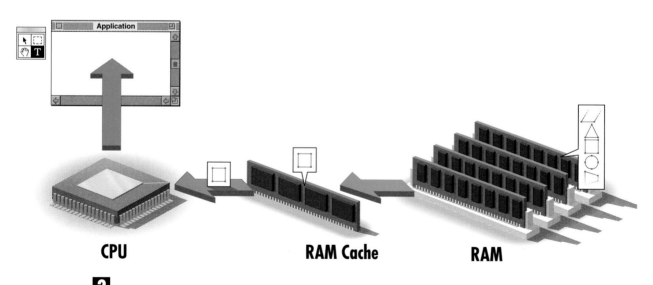

2 RAM passes a copy of the information to the CPU, but it is first intercepted by the cache. The cache makes and keeps a copy, and passes a copy to the CPU.

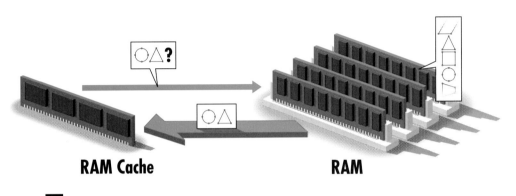

RAM Cache　　　　　　　**RAM**

3 The CPU often requires pieces of information that are grouped together in RAM within a short period of time. When the CPU is not being used, the RAM cache fetches information from the RAM addresses near the addresses of the information last requested by the CPU.

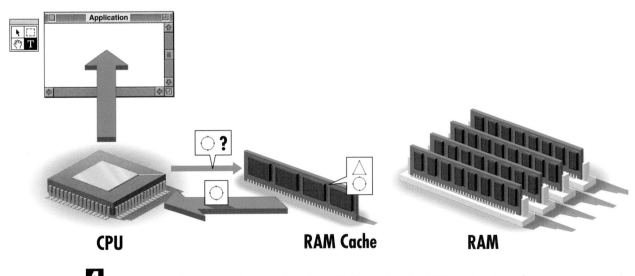

CPU　　　　　**RAM Cache**　　　　**RAM**

4 When the application requires another piece of information, the CPU sends out another query, which once again is intercepted by the cache. This time, the cache has the requested information and sends it along without having to access RAM.

A Disk Cache

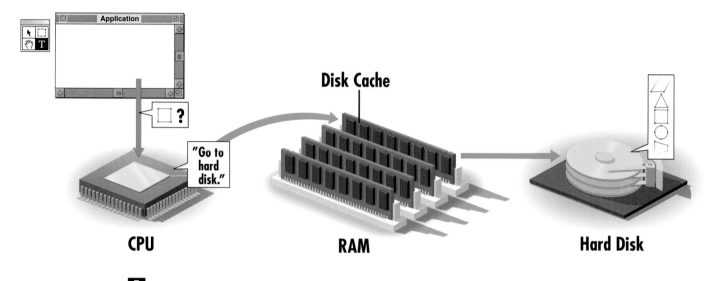

1 System 7 sets aside at least 32K of RAM to be used as a disk cache, although the user can enlarge this. This space is not available to be used as main memory. When an application makes a request for information that is residing on a hard disk, the disk cache intercepts the request and searches itself for the information. If it does not have the requested information, it passes the query along to the disk.

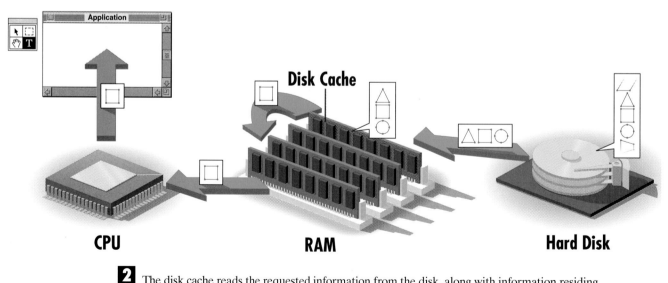

2 The disk cache reads the requested information from the disk, along with information residing in nearby addresses. The disk cache stores the fetched information in its portion of RAM and copies the requested information into main memory, where it is retrieved by the CPU.

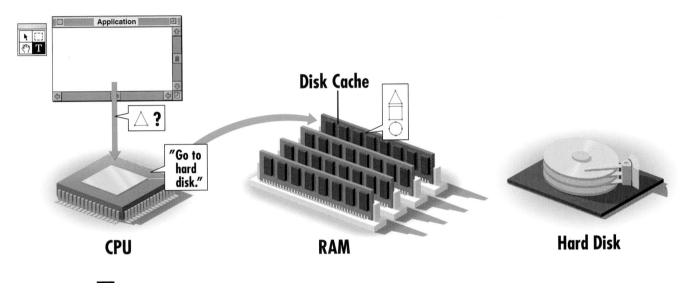

3 When the application requires another piece of information, the CPU sends out another query, which once again is intercepted by the cache.

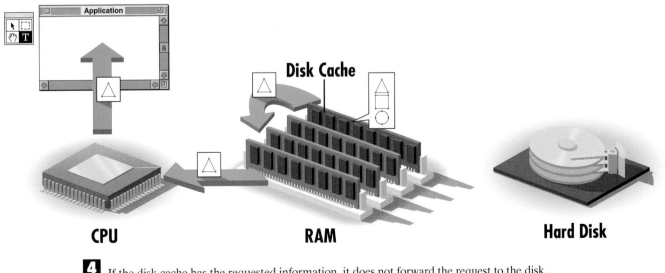

4 If the disk cache has the requested information, it does not forward the request to the disk. Instead, the disk cache copies the information into main memory, where it is retrieved by the CPU.

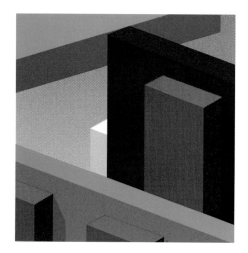

How a RAM Disk Works

A *RAM DISK,* sometimes called a *virtual disk,* is the flip side of virtual memory. Whereas virtual memory takes away a part of a disk and uses it as RAM, a RAM disk takes away part of RAM and uses it as a bootable, desktop-mountable disk. Some PowerBook and desktop models have the ability to create a RAM disk via the Memory control panel. You can also buy add-on RAM disks as expansion boards or external devices. Either way, a RAM disk gives you the speed of RAM with the easy accessibility of a disk drive.

One way to get an idea of the comparative performance of RAM disks and disk drives is to look at the *seek time,* which is the time it takes the storage device to locate a piece of data within it. For moderately fast hard-disk drives, the seek time is usually in the 10- to 15-millisecond range. Because RAM has no moving parts, a RAM disk's seek time is almost zero. Yet, to the user, a RAM disk looks and acts like an ordinary disk drive; you can mount it on the desktop and drag files to and from it. Unfortunately, there is a down side: RAM-disk devices are at least ten times more expensive per megabyte than disk drives.

The principle behind the RAM disk is similar to that of a disk cache (discussed in Chapter 13). A disk cache also takes part of RAM, but the user can't access a disk cache directly, as one can with a RAM disk. The data stored in a RAM disk is not as temporary as data in a cache, which starts erasing old data as soon as it fills up. However, RAM-disk data is not as permanent as disk-drive data, since a RAM disk loses everything stored within it when the computer's power is shut off.

There are several ways to get around this problem. With a PowerBook, you can simply put your Mac in sleep mode instead of turning it off. This keeps power going to the RAM disk while turning off the hard drive and display. However, since a system crash will erase the RAM disk, it is vital that you back up the data on a RAM disk before you put a PowerBook to sleep. Some third-party vendors offer software that will load specific files from a hard-disk drive to a RAM disk every time you start up. External devices sometimes provide an uninterruptable power supply that will continue providing power when you shut down the Mac and for a short time after a power failure.

RAM Disk

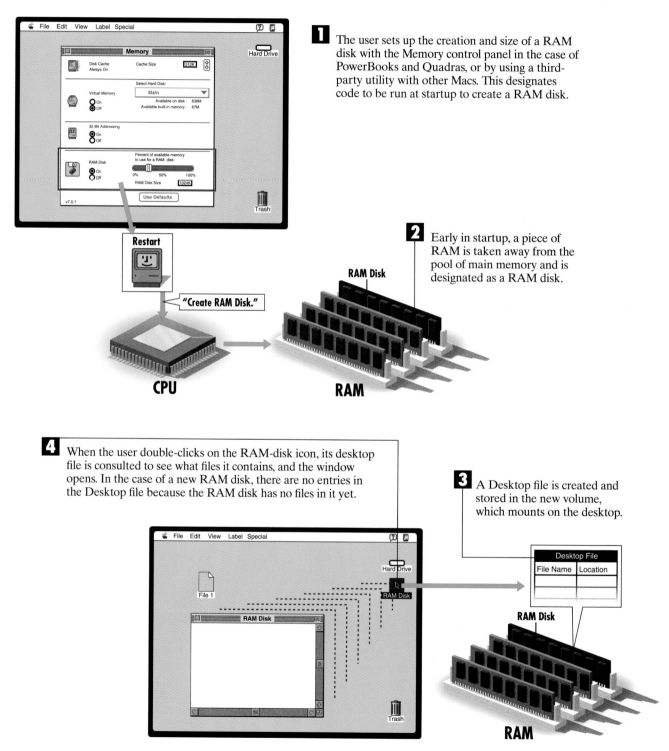

1 The user sets up the creation and size of a RAM disk with the Memory control panel in the case of PowerBooks and Quadras, or by using a third-party utility with other Macs. This designates code to be run at startup to create a RAM disk.

2 Early in startup, a piece of RAM is taken away from the pool of main memory and is designated as a RAM disk.

4 When the user double-clicks on the RAM-disk icon, its desktop file is consulted to see what files it contains, and the window opens. In the case of a new RAM disk, there are no entries in the Desktop file because the RAM disk has no files in it yet.

3 A Desktop file is created and stored in the new volume, which mounts on the desktop.

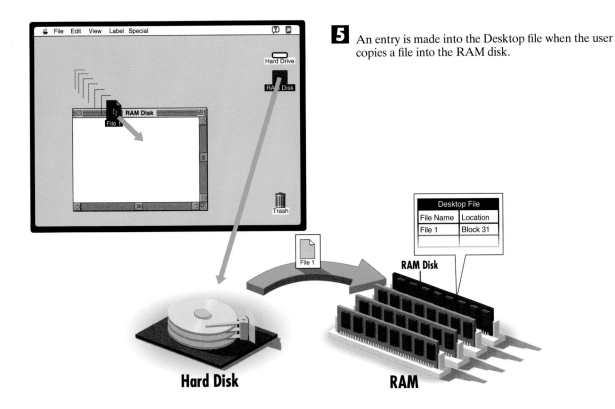

5 An entry is made into the Desktop file when the user copies a file into the RAM disk.

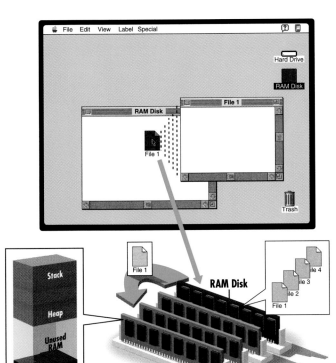

6 Double-clicking on a file in a RAM disk loads the file from the RAM-disk portion into real RAM. The RAM disk stores the file like a document, just as disk drives do, rather than in the stack/heap format of an application's partition in main memory.

MAC FACT To get the most out of a RAM disk, keep a copy of the application you use most frequently and a small System folder on it, and make it the startup disk. Because the System folder contains resources used by applications, putting a System folder on the RAM disk prevents the application from accessing the hard disk, thus improving overall performance.

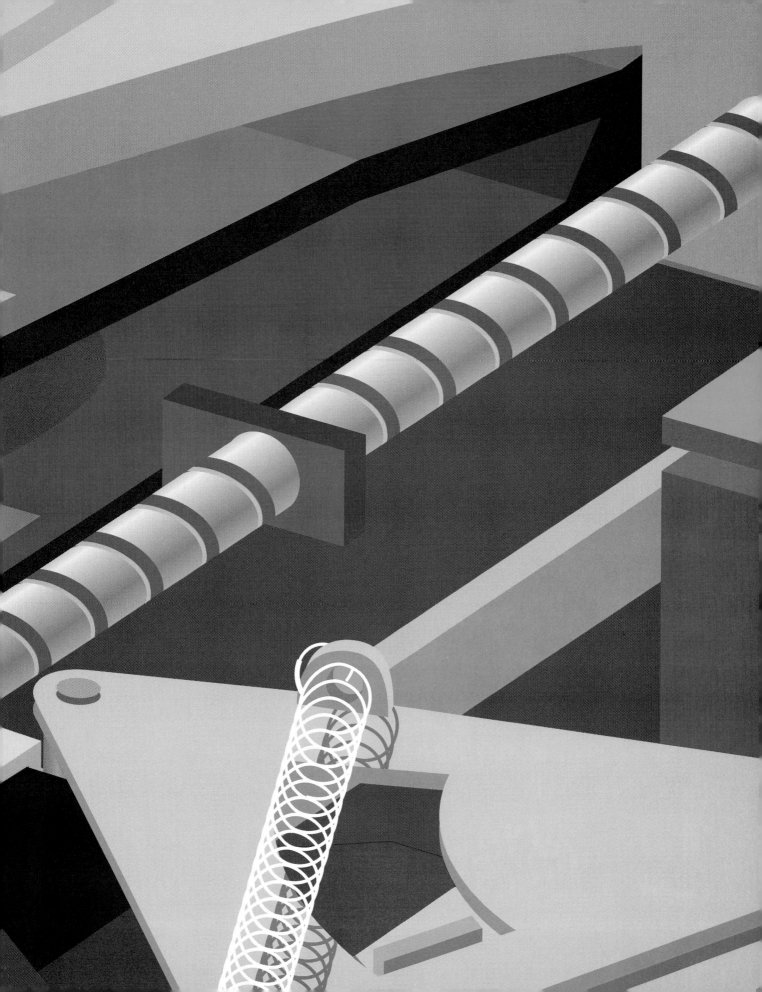

DISK STORAGE

CONTENTS

OVERVIEW

RAM, THE MAC'S short-term memory, holds information only as long as an open application needs it; it is wiped clean every time you shut down the Mac. The Mac's long-term memory, the spinning disks inside disk drives, supplies RAM with the information it needs.

To the CPU, disk drives are secondary storage; to the user, disks are primary storage, the electronic filing cabinets for your applications and data files. (Tape drives, used for backing up disk data, are sometimes called tertiary storage.) Disk drives come in a variety of sizes, capacities, and performance capabilities, and they serve different purposes for the user. Some disks, such as floppies and CD-ROMs, can be removed from the drive for easy transporting. Others, such as hard disks, are an integral part of the drive and cannot be removed.

For convenience, nothing beats a floppy. Portable and cheap, the floppy disk fits in a shirt pocket and costs less than bus fare in most cities. The floppy disk is the Mac's oldest storage medium and still the major method for the distribution of software.

Hard-disk drives are the workhorses of mass storage. Because of their high performance, hard disks are the main place you keep your data, applications, and system software. Hard disks are also available with some of the biggest capacities of any storage devices. Although the original Mac didn't have a hard disk—the System folder and applications could fit on a single 400K disk—hard disks have been standard equipment on Macs for many years.

Floppy and hard disks are both made of magnetic media; the 1s and 0s that make up the data are written and read by electromagnets. A second type of disk media is optical in nature, using laser light to read and write data. Optical media is immune to the deleterious effects of stray magnetic fields, which can corrupt or erase data on magnetic media. The most common types of optical discs are CD-ROM, which is a read-only distribution medium that can hold hundreds of times more data than a floppy disk, and erasable optical discs, which act much like a hard disk.

Regardless of their differences, all mass storage devices behave similarly when connected to a Mac. They can all be mounted on the Finder's desktop as *volumes,* which are icons that appear at the root level of the desktop. With any disk, whether floppy or erasable optical, you can use the Finder to view and access files and folders located on the disk. This is because the operating system's File Manager arranges data on all disks using the same strategy, a method called the hierarchical file system (HFS). If you insert a non-HFS disk, such as a floppy disk formatted for DOS, the Finder won't recognize it and will ask you to eject it. However, utilities from Apple and third-party vendors enable the Finder to recognize and mount non-HFS disks.

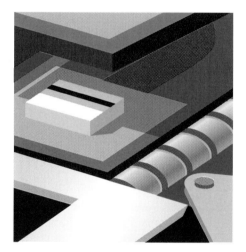

How a Floppy-Disk Drive Works

AT FIRST GLANCE, a Mac floppy disk (known more demurely as a "diskette") is a 3 ½-inch square piece of stiff plastic, appearing to be neither floppy nor disk shaped. However, if you break open the plastic case, you will find a thin, flexible, plastic disk that is indeed floppy.

There are three types of floppy disks the Mac can use. The Mac's original floppy was a single-sided disk that held 400K. Although today's Macs can read 400K disks, the single-sided disks are now mostly an historical artifact. Apple replaced the 400K disk drive in the Mac 512KE with a drive that reads a double-sided 800K disk, which is still in use today. The third type of floppy, the double-sided, double-density disk, holds 1.44MB. Apple started shipping 1.44MB floppy-disk drives in the middle of the Mac SE's production run, and all Macs since then have contained the double-density drives. The 1.44MB floppy-disk drive can also read and write to 800K and 400K disks, as well as to non-HFS floppies formatted for DOS.

Floppy-disk drives have been standard equipment in Macs since the first Mac. Some of the older Mac models have two internal floppy drives, and some Macs have an external floppy port to connect an additional floppy-disk drive. Some PowerBook models don't contain internal floppy-disk drives, but they can connect to an external drive.

Even in today's Macs, floppy disks aren't known for their speed. Floppy disks spin at a much slower rate than hard disks and are connected to the logic board via a serial connection, which sends data one bit at a time. Mechanically, however, floppy-disk drives are quite sophisticated. The Mac's internal process for inserting and ejecting floppies resembles the operation of a Rube Goldberg device: a gear moves a lever, which fits into a slot, which releases a spring-loaded pin, which slides a sled, and so on. These machinations support the Mac's automatic ejection feature, which shoots the disk out at you when you drag the floppy icon to the Trash. Of course, nothing works perfectly all the time, so the drive also supports a manual method of ejecting a floppy. Experienced Mac users will recognize this procedure as the paper-clip trick: Insert the end of a paper clip into the small hole at the right side of the floppy-disk drive, and the disk comes out. It's low-tech, but effective.

Mac Floppy-Disk Drive

1 When a floppy disk is inserted correctly, the diagonally cut corner (not shown) on the disk case moves aside a pin on a lever, letting the disk pass farther into the drive. If the disk is inserted backwards or upside down, the pin will hit the straight edge of the disk and prevent it from entering the drive.

2 When the disk is almost inside the drive, the edge of the disk's shutter door hits a pin attached to a spring-loaded lever. As the disk moves farther in, the lever pivots clockwise, pushing the pin to open the metal shutter and exposing the thin, flexible disk inside.

3 This same pivoting lever moves another pin that holds the lower sled in place. With the pin moved, springs move the lower sled toward the front of the drive, causing the spring-loaded upper sled to fall. This moves the floppy below the level of the insertion slot.

Read/write heads

Upper sled

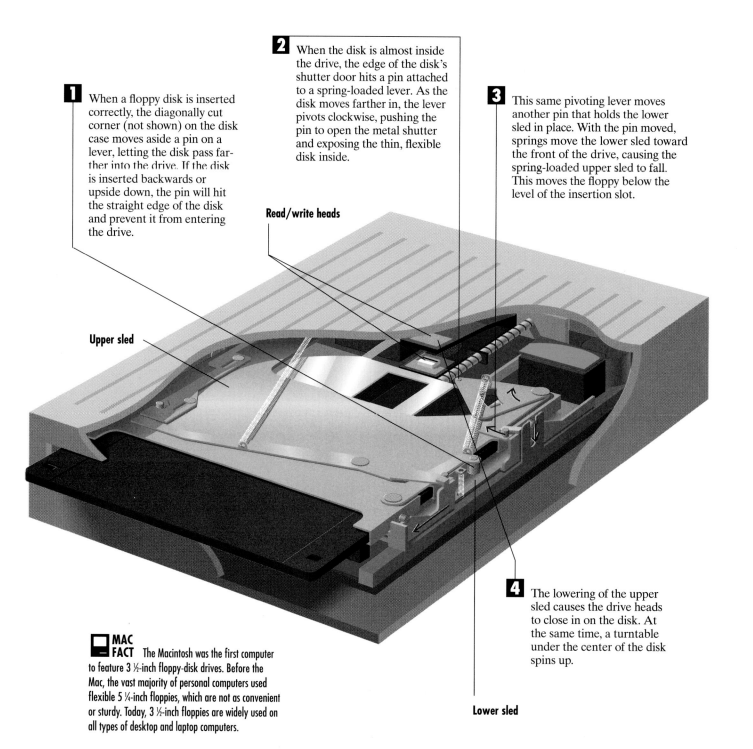

4 The lowering of the upper sled causes the drive heads to close in on the disk. At the same time, a turntable under the center of the disk spins up.

Lower sled

MAC FACT The Macintosh was the first computer to feature 3 ½-inch floppy-disk drives. Before the Mac, the vast majority of personal computers used flexible 5 ¼-inch floppies, which are not as convenient or sturdy. Today, 3 ½-inch floppies are widely used on all types of desktop and laptop computers.

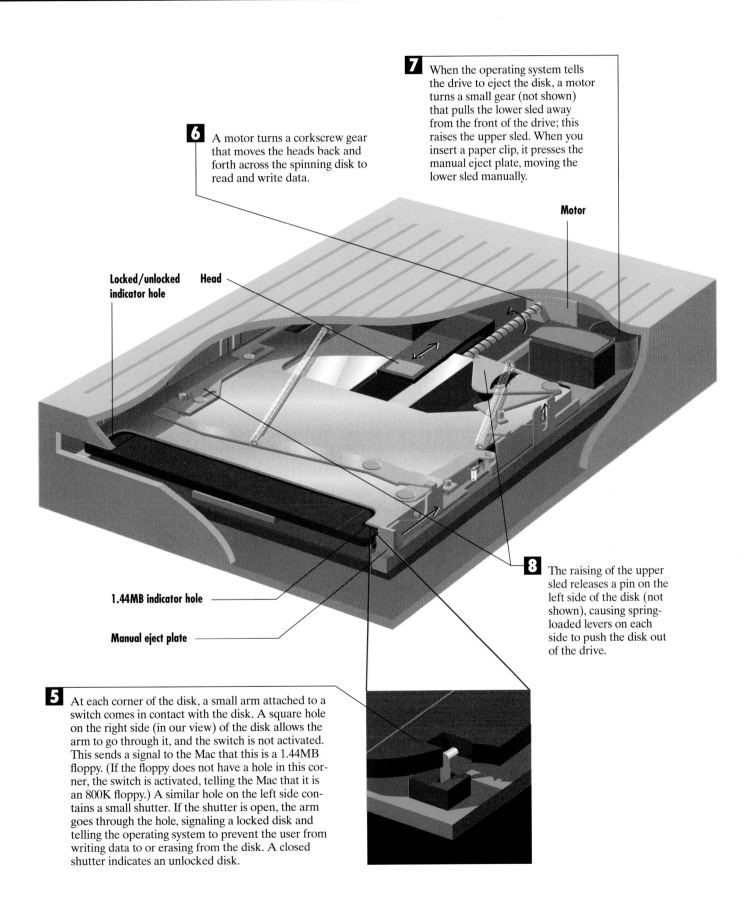

7 When the operating system tells the drive to eject the disk, a motor turns a small gear (not shown) that pulls the lower sled away from the front of the drive; this raises the upper sled. When you insert a paper clip, it presses the manual eject plate, moving the lower sled manually.

Motor

6 A motor turns a corkscrew gear that moves the heads back and forth across the spinning disk to read and write data.

Locked/unlocked indicator hole

Head

1.44MB indicator hole

Manual eject plate

8 The raising of the upper sled releases a pin on the left side of the disk (not shown), causing spring-loaded levers on each side to push the disk out of the drive.

5 At each corner of the disk, a small arm attached to a switch comes in contact with the disk. A square hole on the right side (in our view) of the disk allows the arm to go through it, and the switch is not activated. This sends a signal to the Mac that this is a 1.44MB floppy. (If the floppy does not have a hole in this corner, the switch is activated, telling the Mac that it is an 800K floppy.) A similar hole on the left side contains a small shutter. If the shutter is open, the arm goes through the hole, signaling a locked disk and telling the operating system to prevent the user from writing data to or erasing from the disk. A closed shutter indicates an unlocked disk.

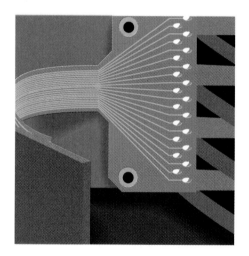

How a Hard-Disk Drive Works

THE HARD-DISK drive is the method of data storage most Mac and PC users continually depend upon to hold and retrieve software and the work we produce. A high-precision machine, the hard-disk drive is the fastest mechanical storage device available, second only to RAM (which is non-mechanical) in speed, but far less expensive.

Inside a humming hard-disk drive are several spinning rigid aluminum platters, coated on both sides with a magnetic material. The coating contains particles of oxides of iron or other magnetic material, which hold the 0s and 1s of binary data. Data is written on the disks by magnetizing areas on the disk surface, similar to the way information is recorded and read on audio and video tape.

The disks spin together at a constant rate somewhere between 3,600 and 5,400 revolutions per minute (rpm), depending on the drive, though new technological advances are enabling manufacturers to build faster drives every year. By comparison, floppy disks spin at variable speeds at around 360 rpm.

Moving rapidly back and forth over the surface of the disks are tiny electromagnets called *heads*, which read and write data. The very high precision of a hard-disk drive is apparent when you consider the fact that a 3 ½-inch disk spinning at 3,600 rpm is passing under the heads at the equivalent of more than 75 miles per hour. Like a car crash at these speeds, a *head crash*, which occurs when a head plows into a platter, is very destructive. A head crash can occur when a platter wobbles due to old age or from a jolt to the drive.

A head crash can also be caused by a speck of dust. The distance between head and platter is only a matter of several dozen microns (millionths of a meter). At this scale, a speck of dust is a huge boulder that can carve a trench in the disk media, ruining swaths of data. To prevent dust getting anywhere near the platters and heads, they are permanently encased in an airtight metal case, which also acts to conduct heat away from the disks.

The platter-and-head assembly is attached to a circuit board containing the drive's controlling electronics, which together are referred to as the hard-disk *mechanism*. The mechanism can be placed directly inside the Mac or in an external case along with a power supply and fan.

Before any data can be written, the disk must be formatted with software to set up the organizational structures in which the data will be arranged on the disk. Formatting also creates information on the disk that is loaded into the Mac at startup. This information helps the Mac locate files stored on the drive.

Hard-Disk Drive Formatting

Standard Formatting

1 When a hard disk is formatted, concentric rings called *tracks* are created on the disk. They are similar to the areas on a phonograph record taken up by individual songs. Tracks on a hard-disk drive are much thinner than audio tracks; hard-disk platters can contain 600 tracks per inch or more.

2 Tracks are physically divided into *sectors,* which are areas that can contain 512 bytes of data each. In standard formatting, sectors are arranged in pie-like slices, so that sectors near the center take up less disk space than sectors near the edge of the disk. However, all sectors contain the same amount of data in standard formatting.

3 The size of a disk determines the size of a *block,* which is the smallest amount of data transferred at one time by the drive. The larger the disk, the larger the block. A block can be one or more whole sectors, but never a fraction of a sector.

4 After laying down the tracks and sectors—which is called *physical formatting*—the formatting software performs logical formatting. *Logical formatting* creates various directories and indexes on the disk that are loaded into the Mac's RAM to tell the Mac where to find files. Logical formatting creates five areas: the boot blocks, the volume information blocks, the extents directory, the catalog tree, and the data area. These "structures" take up disk space, which is why a disk with no files on it will not have its full capacity available to the user.

5 The *boot blocks,* which are always the first two blocks of the disk, identify the disk as a Macintosh disk and contain information used during the startup process. They also contain the SCSI driver, which enables the Mac to communicate with the hard drive over the SCSI bus.

6 The *volume information blocks,* which always follow the boot blocks, contain the volume name (the name you give to your disk) and number of files stored on the disk. This is followed by the volume bitmap, which identifies the used and unused blocks.

Volume bitmap

9 The *data area* takes up most of the disk and is where you store your files.

8 The *catalog tree* is a directory that stores the locations of files on the platters. The Mac Operating System uses the catalog tree to locate files when needed.

7 The *extents directory* contains the location of blocks that are located next to each other, called *contiguous blocks.* When you copy a file to a hard-disk drive, the extents directory looks for contiguous blocks to write the file to.

Partitions

1 Most formatting software can create *partitions*, which are sections of a disk drive that act as separate Mac volumes of a fixed capacity. A disk partitioned into three volumes will appear as three hard-disk icons on the Finder's desktop.

Wasted disk space

10MB partition

30MB partition

60MB partition

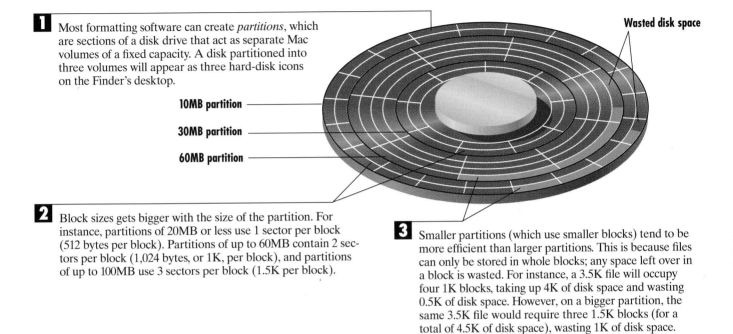

2 Block sizes gets bigger with the size of the partition. For instance, partitions of 20MB or less use 1 sector per block (512 bytes per block). Partitions of up to 60MB contain 2 sectors per block (1,024 bytes, or 1K, per block), and partitions of up to 100MB use 3 sectors per block (1.5K per block).

3 Smaller partitions (which use smaller blocks) tend to be more efficient than larger partitions. This is because files can only be stored in whole blocks; any space left over in a block is wasted. For instance, a 3.5K file will occupy four 1K blocks, taking up 4K of disk space and wasting 0.5K of disk space. However, on a bigger partition, the same 3.5K file would require three 1.5K blocks (for a total of 4.5K of disk space), wasting 1K of disk space.

Banded Formatting

1 A newer type of formatting, called *banded*, or *zone bit*, *formatting*, can pack more sectors on a disk and provide faster performance. It does this by making sector sizes on the outside track just as small (and just as dense) as the sectors on the inside tracks.

3 Since the platters rotate at a constant rate, more sectors pass under the heads at the outside tracks during each revolution than do at the inside tracks, which means the data on the outside tracks can be accessed at a faster rate.

2 This leads to more sectors (and therefore, more data) on the outside tracks than on the inside tracks. A file that takes up about half of an inside track requires less than one-fourth of an outside track.

MAC FACT Some advanced formatting software will let you specify the size of blocks, so you can keep them small on large partitions. However, small blocks on large partitions can slow down performance with certain applications due to the processing overhead of keeping track of more blocks. With banded formatting, optimization utilities are available that move your system and application files to the faster outer tracks for better overall performance.

Hard-Disk Operation

3 The drive's logic board sends an electric current to the head actuator motor to move the heads rapidly back and forth over the spinning platters. All the heads are connected to the same actuator, and they move in unison. The actuator is held by a spring. When the current increases, the heads move toward the center of the spinning disks. When the current decreases, the spring pulls the heads back toward the outer edge of the disks.

2 Some drives store incoming write commands in a write cache to speed up performance. The *write cache* holds the write command while telling the Mac's CPU that the task has been completed, and it writes the data when it gets a chance. The benefit is that the CPU doesn't have to wait for the actual writing to take place before sending more commands.

4 Sector boundaries are marked by strongly magnetized lines. The heads count these boundaries to determine which sector they are currently over and to keep from wandering from correct locations.

1 A command comes in from the SCSI bus ordering the drive to perform a task, such as writing data to the disk. The command is received by the drive's controller circuitry on the logic board, which processes the command.

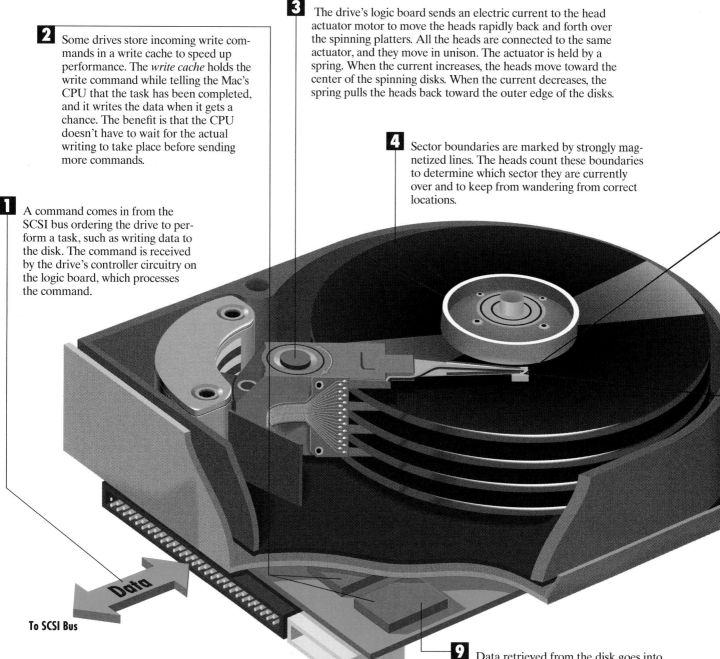

Data

To SCSI Bus

9 Data retrieved from the disk goes into the drive cache, which saves the most recently requested information. If the Mac asks for information that is already in the cache, the drive sends the data without having to access the platters.

5 When the specified sector passes under a head, a current flows through the coil to produce a magnetic field, turning the head into a magnet. The head magnetizes a small area of the disk under the head, so that "north" poles of the magnetic particles in the area are all facing in one direction. This magnetized area represents 1 bit.

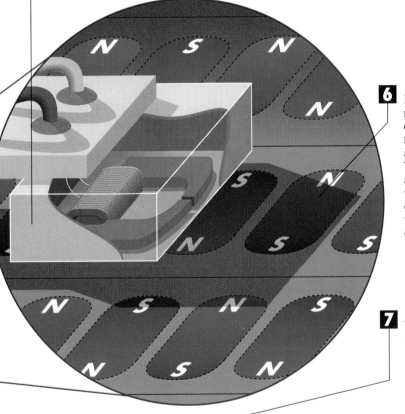

6 Reversing the direction of the current in the coil under another area on the platter reverses the magnetic field, causing the north pole of the area to face the opposite direction. The two oppositely magnetized areas represent 0s and 1s. An area with a north pole oriented in one direction represents a 1, and an area with a north pole oriented in the opposite direction represents a 0.

7 The volume bitmap, now in RAM, is used to locate free blocks on the disk. The extents tree looks for blocks that are next to each other to write the file. If most of the files on the disk are stored in noncontiguous blocks, the disk is said to be fragmented. A fragmented disk is slower since the heads must move farther between blocks when reading a file. Disk optimization software can defragment a disk by moving data around so that files are contiguous.

8 Reading data is the reverse of the above process: The catalog directory loaded into RAM is used to find the blocks on the disks where the data is stored. When the heads pass over the magnetized bits, a current is produced in the coil. Current flowing in one direction is read as a 0, while current produced in the opposite direction is read as a 1. This technique of moving magnetic material near wire coils to produce an electric current exploits the same electromagnetic phenomena used to produce electricity in power plants.

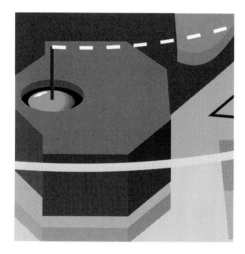

CHAPTER

How Optical-Disc Drives Work

REPLACE THE PRECISION mechanics of a hard-disk drive with the precision optics of a laser-guided telemetry system and you have the basis for optical storage. Optical-disc drives use a series of lenses and mirrors to guide a tiny laser beam to microscopic areas on a single rotating disc. The precise aiming of the laser enables data bits to be written much closer together than on hard-disk platters, so that one side of an optical disc can hold as much data as six double-sided magnetic platters.

There are two major types of optical storage device in use today. *Magneto-optical storage,* also called erasable optical storage, allows you to read and write data, as you do with a hard or floppy disk. *CD-ROM* (compact disc read-only memory), based on CD audio technology, is used for distributing software, data, and multimedia presentations.

Both types use removable discs. Erasable optical discs come in two standard sizes, 5 ¼ inch, which can hold up to 1.3 gigabytes of information, and 3 ½ inch, which can hold up to 250MB. CD-ROM discs look like audio CDs and can hold up to 600MB of data. In addition to data discs, today's CD-ROM drives can read audio CDs and Kodak's Photo CDs, which hold digital images of photographs.

Optical storage is a safer, more durable method of storage than magnetic disks or tape. Whereas it is not uncommon for hard-disk drives to fail after five years, magneto-optical media is estimated to hold data for at least 30 years and can sustain 10 million read/write cycles. The estimated lifespan for CD-ROM is 100 years, making it an attractive alternative to film-based storage, such as microfiche and microfilm.

During operation, optical read/write heads are much farther away from the media than are hard-drive heads, so head crashes are rare. And although lenses can become dirty over time, dust cannot harm the mechanism, as it can with hard-disk drives. Optical media is also immune to magnetic fields, which can erase data on hard and floppy disks.

When you need to store hundreds of megabytes of data, optical storage is cheaper than hard-disk storage. CD-ROM, which can hold the equivalent of 200,000 pages of text, is even less expensive than paper. There is one drawback: performance. The fastest erasable optical drives are two or three times slower than the best hard-disk drives, and CD-ROM is about ten times slower. For this reason, optical drives are mostly used to augment magnetic storage, not to replace it.

Magneto-optical Storage

1 Magneto-optical discs are encased in a protective cartridge much like that on a floppy disk, only bigger. When the cartridge is inserted in the drive, the disk spins at a constant speed of 3,000 rpm or more, depending on the drive.

2 To write data, the drive uses an electromagnet and a laser head positioned on opposite sides of the disc. (Hence the term magneto-optical.) The head slides back and forth over the disc on a sled until it is located over the appropriate track.

4 The laser light passes through a layer of protective plastic (or sometimes glass), which is about 1.2 millimeters thick, to the recording layer of the disc. This layer contains a special magnetic material that can change its magnetic polarity only at temperatures above 150 degrees centigrade. To write a bit of data, the laser heats a spot for a short time—about 800 nanoseconds (billionths of a second).

3 The lens head directs a beam of light from a laser diode through a series of lenses and mirrors. Photosensitive detectors are used to check for accurate positioning of the head and to read data.

5 At the same time, the electromagnet turns on, creating a magnetic field surrounding the area on the disc representing a bit. Only the bit at 150 degrees centigrade is affected by the magnet.

Direction of disk motion

6 To write data, two passes must be made: an erase pass and a write pass. During the erase pass, the magnet is turned on and all bits become magnetized with their north poles facing down, representing all 0s.

7 During the write pass, the magnet switches polarity so that the north pole faces up. Bits that need to be changed to 1 are heated with the laser, and their polarity is reversed by the magnet. Bits that are to remain 0 are not heated, and are therefore unaffected by the magnet.

8 A much less powerful laser beam is used for reading data. The light passes through the protective and recording layers and bounces off of the reflective layer back toward the head. The laser light is polarized, meaning that the light waves are all oriented in one direction. As this polarized light passes through the recording layer, the magnetic material rotates the direction of the light waves. Bits magnetized as a 1 rotate the light clockwise, and 0 bits rotate the light counterclockwise. The photosensitive detectors can recognize the difference.

Detector

MAC FACT Although both sides of a 3 ½-inch optical cartridge can be accessed inside the drive, you need to eject a 5 ¼-inch cartridge, flip it over, and reinsert it to read data on the opposite side. Otherwise, most magneto-optical discs act a lot like giant floppy disks: Pop the cartridge in the drive, and the disc volume mounts on the desktop. Drag the icon to the Trash, and the cartridge ejects from the drive.

CD-ROM Storage

1 A CD-ROM disc is placed in a protective tray called a caddy, which is inserted into the drive. Data is read from the bottom side of the disc.

2 The read head moves on a sled back and forth under the disc and directs a beam of light from a laser diode through a series of lenses and mirrors.

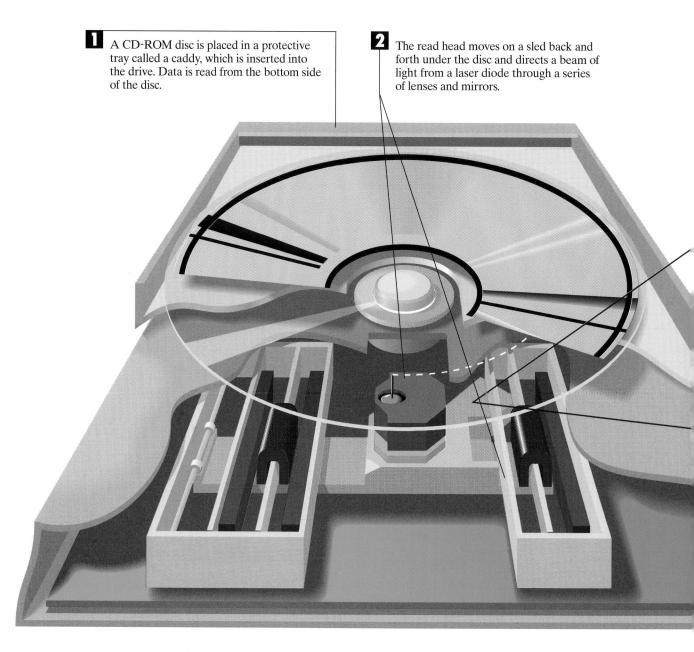

MAC FACT Many commercially available CD-ROM discs can be run on both Macs and PCs because the data is written in a standard format that both operating systems can understand. The first multiplatform CD-ROM standard is called High Sierra because it was hammered out by a group of manufacturers and software publishers near Lake Tahoe, California, in the Sierra Nevada Mountains. High Sierra was later formalized in an international standard called ISO 9660.

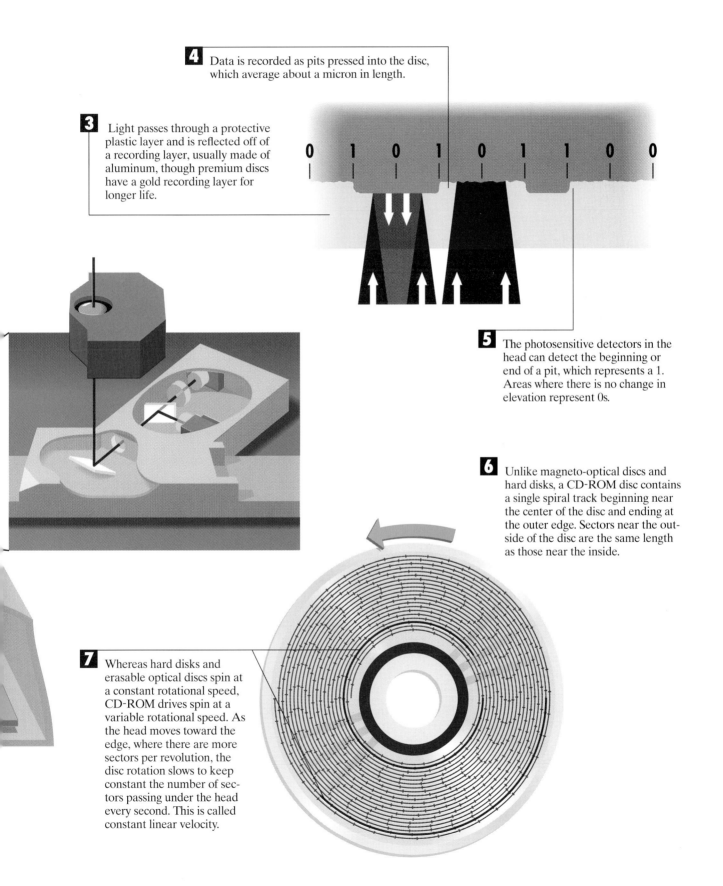

4 Data is recorded as pits pressed into the disc, which average about a micron in length.

3 Light passes through a protective plastic layer and is reflected off of a recording layer, usually made of aluminum, though premium discs have a gold recording layer for longer life.

0   1   0   1   0   1   1   0   0

5 The photosensitive detectors in the head can detect the beginning or end of a pit, which represents a 1. Areas where there is no change in elevation represent 0s.

6 Unlike magneto-optical discs and hard disks, a CD-ROM disc contains a single spiral track beginning near the center of the disc and ending at the outer edge. Sectors near the outside of the disc are the same length as those near the inside.

7 Whereas hard disks and erasable optical discs spin at a constant rotational speed, CD-ROM drives spin at a variable rotational speed. As the head moves toward the edge, where there are more sectors per revolution, the disc rotation slows to keep constant the number of sectors passing under the head every second. This is called constant linear velocity.

GETTING INFORMATION IN AND OUT

CONTENTS

ONNECTED TO THE back of the Mac through an often tangled spaghetti of cables are the peripheral devices that enable us to have a two-way conversation with the Mac's CPU. We send commands and data through keyboards, scanners, and microphones, and the Mac responds through video monitors, printers, and speakers. These are the hands, eyes, and ears of the Mac, known in tech-speak as input/output, or simply I/O.

Other add-on devices give new capabilities to the Mac. Hard-disk and optical-disc drives give you the ability to store more data files, and internal accelerators or video cards can give you faster processing or support for a bigger monitor. However, to the CPU and RAM, it doesn't matter what type of device is connected—it's all I/O to them.

The various devices we can connect to a Mac plug into several different types of *ports*, which consist of a connector and circuitry on the logic board that sends and receives signals to the devices. Expansion cards connect to an expansion slot, which is really just a port that is on the inside of the Mac. Both internal and external I/O devices plug into connectors on the Mac's logic board.

The connectors on different ports are shaped differently from each other to prevent users from plugging the wrong device into the wrong port. Not only would a device not work if plugged into the wrong port, but both it and the Mac's circuitry would be harmed as well. This is because not all ports are alike. Each type of port sends and receives information in a different manner.

The ports on a Mac can be categorized as two types: a single-device port, to which you can add one device; and a bus, which connects multiple devices through multiple connectors or by daisy-chaining. A bus is like a simple network, where one device at a time can connect to the communications line. The bus on the Mac includes the NuBus expansion slots, the SCSI port for hard disks, and the Apple Desktop Bus (ADB) ports for keyboards and mice. The printer, modem, and sound ports, and the processor direct slot (PDS) are direct ports supporting a single device each.

The different types of signals running back and forth across these ports are translated into a form the CPU and RAM can read by the port circuitry on the Mac's logic board. All the ports are connected to the CPU and RAM via the system bus, a data highway on the logic board that connects other parts of the Mac as well. Traffic flowing in and out of the Mac across the system bus and out to the devices is directed by the various managers in the operating system.

A key feature of all ports and expansion slots on the Mac is ease of setup. Installing a peripheral device usually involves nothing more than plugging it in and sometimes dragging some files to the System folder. Usually there are no DIP switches to set or jumpers to remove. The design of the ports has more to do with the ease of setup than with the design of the devices themselves.

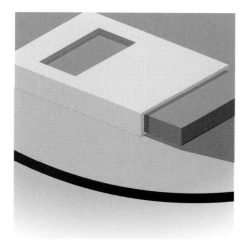

CHAPTER
18

How SCSI Works

EVERY MAC SINCE the Mac Plus has had the ability to use not just one hard disk, but up to seven devices through a single port at the back of the Mac—the SCSI port. SCSI (pronounced *scuzzy*) stands for Small Computer System Interface, and it is an industry standard for connecting peripherals, such as internal and external hard-disk and optical-disc drives, scanners, and non-network printers. SCSI lets you plug a peripheral into the back of the last peripheral of your SCSI chain rather than using a port or add-in card for each device. This is because SCSI is technically a *bus*, a common pathway shared by multiple devices.

Before the Mac Plus, the only way you could connect a hard disk to a Mac was via a *serial connection,* which sends one bit at a time. SCSI is significantly faster than a serial connection because it is a *parallel connection,* transferring a whole byte (8 bits) at a time.

Signals from the Mac are sent out on the SCSI bus by the operating system's SCSI Manager, which commands the SCSI controller chip on the Mac's logic board. Each peripheral has a SCSI driver that is loaded into the Mac's system partition in RAM at startup. With the drivers loaded into the Mac's RAM, the Mac knows which devices to look for on the SCSI bus.

A *terminating resistor* is required on the first and last devices on the bus to identify the extent of the bus and to prevent signals from reflecting back on the bus after reaching the last device. The terminator is usually plugged into a device's SCSI connector, though some hard drives have internal terminators. The Mac supplies termination for internal disk drives. Power (5 volts) for the resistor is supplied by the peripheral, not the Mac.

The American National Standards Institute (ANSI) has revised the SCSI standard with a new specification called SCSI 2, which is compatible with older SCSI devices. SCSI 2 uses a variety of methods to improve performance. Apple has implemented parts of SCSI 2 in its newer, high-end Macs, and third-party vendors offer add-in cards that provide further speed enhancements.

SCSI Chain

1 When a user drags a file from the floppy drive to a hard disk, the SCSI Manager tells the SCSI controller chip to initiate a SCSI transfer. The SCSI controller treats the Mac logic board—including CPU, RAM, and floppy drive—as a device with SCSI ID 7. An internal hard disk is treated as a separate SCSI device, usually (but not always) with the SCSI ID 0.

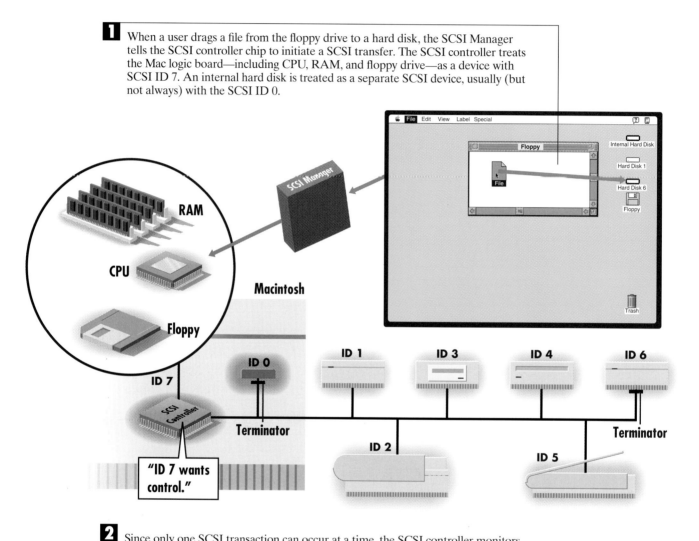

2 Since only one SCSI transaction can occur at a time, the SCSI controller monitors for a free bus. If it detects a transaction occurring, it waits. When it hears nothing, the SCSI controller sends out a signal to gain control of the bus. If no termination signal is detected, it will not be able to see any of the other SCSI devices. If more than one SCSI device seeks control at the same time, the one with the highest number wins. Since the Mac has the highest possible ID, it always wins.

MAC FACT SCSI was designed to be a plug-and-play method of adding storage devices to the Mac, but it is temperamental, particularly when you have multiple devices on the bus. Next to proper termination, cables play the biggest role in setting up a SCSI chain that works. Using cables that are more heavily shielded inside helps ensure signal integrity. It also helps if none of the cables are longer than 3 feet. Problems can also arise if you disconnect SCSI devices while the Mac is turned on.

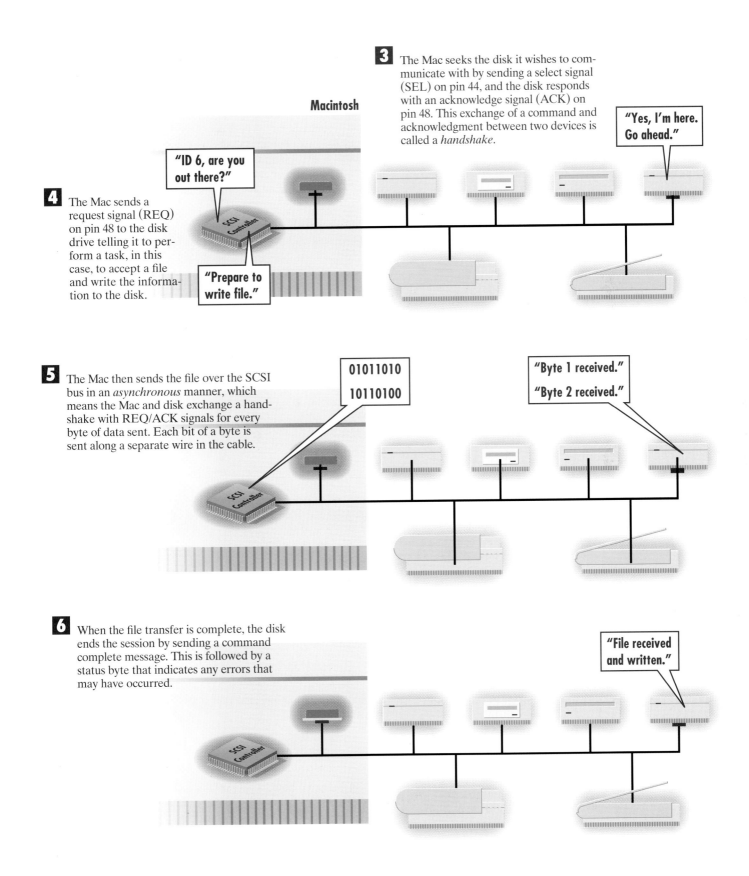

3 The Mac seeks the disk it wishes to communicate with by sending a select signal (SEL) on pin 44, and the disk responds with an acknowledge signal (ACK) on pin 48. This exchange of a command and acknowledgment between two devices is called a *handshake*.

"Yes, I'm here. Go ahead."

Macintosh

"ID 6, are you out there?"

4 The Mac sends a request signal (REQ) on pin 48 to the disk drive telling it to perform a task, in this case, to accept a file and write the information to the disk.

"Prepare to write file."

5 The Mac then sends the file over the SCSI bus in an *asynchronous* manner, which means the Mac and disk exchange a handshake with REQ/ACK signals for every byte of data sent. Each bit of a byte is sent along a separate wire in the cable.

01011010
10110100

"Byte 1 received."
"Byte 2 received."

6 When the file transfer is complete, the disk ends the session by sending a command complete message. This is followed by a status byte that indicates any errors that may have occurred.

"File received and written."

How the Apple Desktop Bus Works

BECAUSE THEY ARE the primary data-entry and control devices, the keyboard and the mouse are the peripherals you spend the most time with. Since the introduction of the Mac SE in 1987, all Macs have used the Apple Desktop Bus, or ADB, to connect the computer to the mouse and keyboard. Some Macs have a single ADB port, though most models have two.

ADB offers a big advantage over the keyboard port of the earlier models, in that you can daisy-chain input devices from one to the other, connecting more devices than the number of ports. This lets you plug in multiple keyboards or mice, as well as trackballs and pen tablets. ADB can theoretically support up to 16 devices, but Apple recommends no more than 3 devices per port for optimal performance.

All ADB devices, even those connected to different ADB ports, communicate over a single bus. Each device has a unique identifying address, and messages can be sent to more than one address at the same time. Unlike other buses, all devices on ADB are not created equal. The Mac is the boss and can't be interrupted. If a device wants attention, it must ask the Mac for permission to speak.

Like a local area network, ADB uses a data transmission method called asynchronous serial communications. *Asynchronous* means that bytes of data aren't sent automatically according to a timed sequence, but instead are sent when a response is received from the target device. *Serial* means that each bit in a byte is sent one after the other, instead of at the same time, as in a parallel bus such as SCSI.

The ADB is not a particularly fast port, but the amount of data being transferred is minuscule compared to the data handled by a SCSI bus—the ADB transfers single characters at a time instead of whole pages of text or graphics. What ADB lacks in performance it makes up for in simplicity and ease of use. The connector contains a mere four pins: one to send the ADB signals, one to supply 5 volts to power the ADB devices, a third to act as a ground, and a fourth to enable the user to start up the Mac from the keyboard.

The Apple Desktop Bus

Every Mac has a single Apple Desktop Bus (even those with two ADB ports), which uses asynchronous communications among all connected devices. The Mac logic board and each input device contain an ADB transceiver chip, which converts bus signals to something the devices can understand. The Mac also has one or more Versatile Interface Adapter (*VIA*) chips, which handle most of the trade of information between the CPU and RAM and the ports and storage devices. ADB devices contain a microprocessor and a small amount of memory to hold user commands until they can be transferred to the Mac.

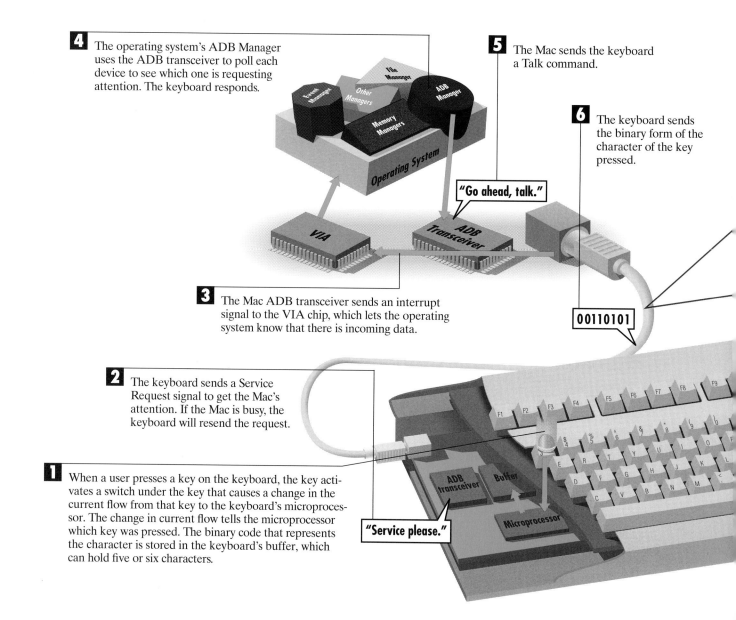

4 The operating system's ADB Manager uses the ADB transceiver to poll each device to see which one is requesting attention. The keyboard responds.

5 The Mac sends the keyboard a Talk command.

6 The keyboard sends the binary form of the character of the key pressed.

"Go ahead, talk."

3 The Mac ADB transceiver sends an interrupt signal to the VIA chip, which lets the operating system know that there is incoming data.

00110101

2 The keyboard sends a Service Request signal to get the Mac's attention. If the Mac is busy, the keyboard will resend the request.

1 When a user presses a key on the keyboard, the key activates a switch under the key that causes a change in the current flow from that key to the keyboard's microprocessor. The change in current flow tells the microprocessor which key was pressed. The binary code that represents the character is stored in the keyboard's buffer, which can hold five or six characters.

"Service please."

8 The ADB transceiver in the Mac receives the keypress and passes it to the VIA, which sends a message to the operating system's Event Manager. This message is then passed on to the Toolbox Event Manager. Finally, the key is displayed on screen as a character or, if the user pressed a key combination, a command is carried out. The Mac will regularly poll the keyboard for additional data until another device sends a service rquest.

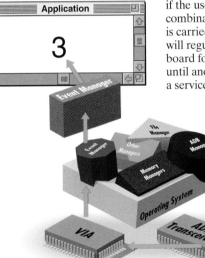

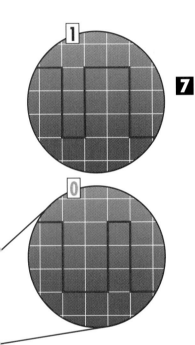

7 A data bit is sent as a low voltage followed by a high voltage. A 0 is represented by a long low voltage (65 microseconds) followed by a short high voltage. A 1 is represented by a short low voltage (35 microseconds) followed by a long high voltage. Commands also use this scheme, varying the lengths of the voltages in different ways.

MAC FACT Pre-ADB Macs (the original 128K Mac to the Mac Plus) used two separate ports for the mouse and keyboard. The keyboard port used *synchronous* transmission, in which data signals were sent on a timed schedule according to a clock on the logic board. Although users could add a separate numeric keypad to the Mac Plus keyboard, daisy-chaining of devices was prevented by the need to perform the complex task of synchronizing signals from multiple devices. Synchronous communication was abandoned in favor of the asynchronous approach of ADB in the Mac SE and the non-Mac Apple IIGS.

ADB Mouse

1 Two capstans at right angles to each other are in contact with a rubber-coated steel ball that partially protrudes from the bottom of the mouse. When you move the mouse, the ball rotates the two capstans, which measure the up-and-down and side-to-side motion of the mouse, as well as the speed of the mouse in each direction.

2 Each capstan turns an interrupt wheel, a disk with 24 slots. For each slotted wheel, a tiny infrared lamp sends a beam of light through the moving wheels to a detector on the other side of the wheel. When a slot lines up with a lamp and detector, the beam is received, and an electrical pulse is generated. When a slot does not, it blocks the light, and no pulse is generated. These pulse signals are sent to the mouse's microprocessor.

Mouse button switch

Capstan

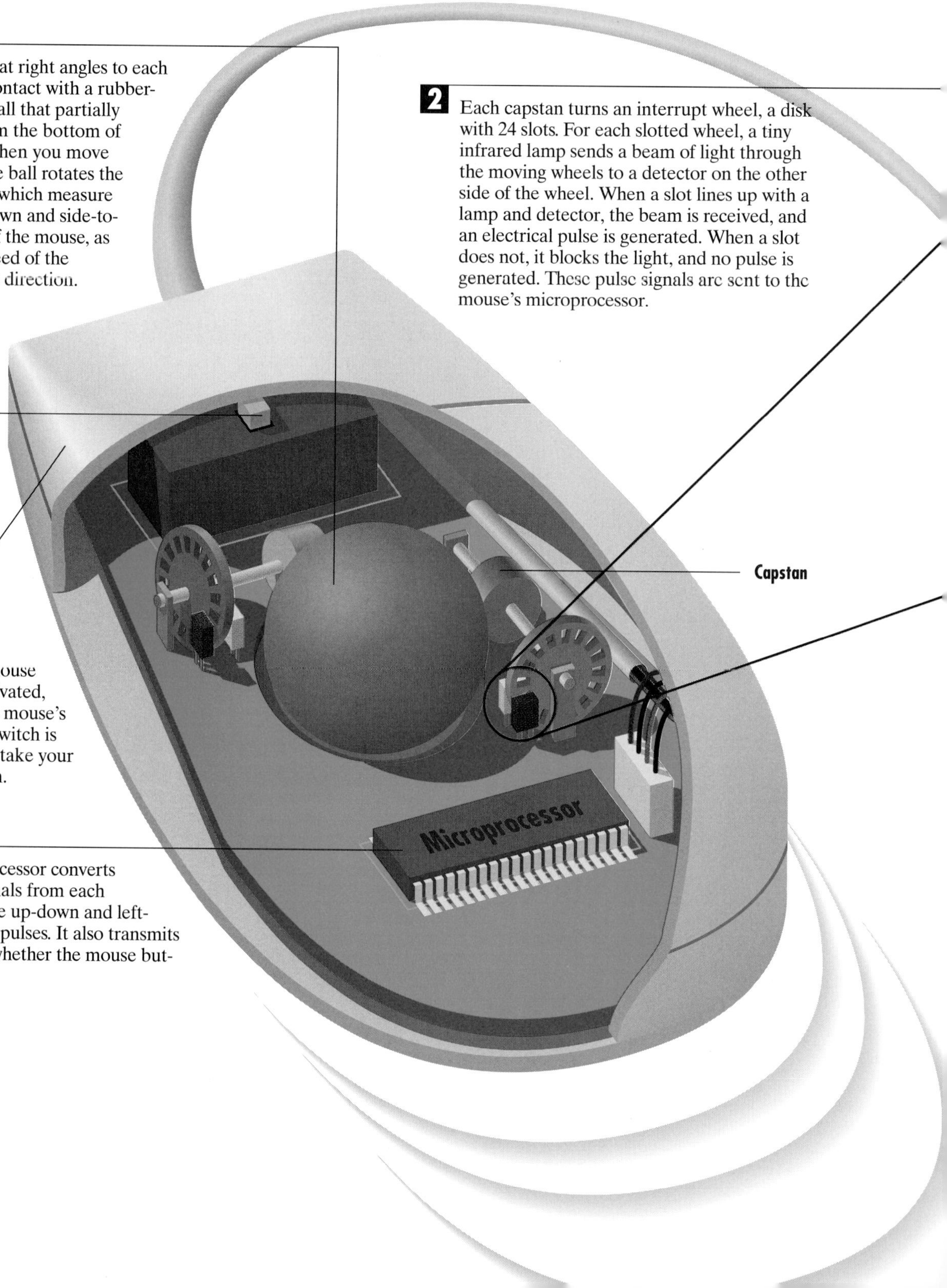

3 When you press the mouse button, a switch is activated, sending a signal to the mouse's microprocessor. The switch is deactivated when you take your finger off of the button.

Microprocessor

4 The mouse's microprocessor converts the lamp/detector signals from each wheel, representing the up-down and left-right motion, to ADB pulses. It also transmits a signal representing whether the mouse button is up or down.

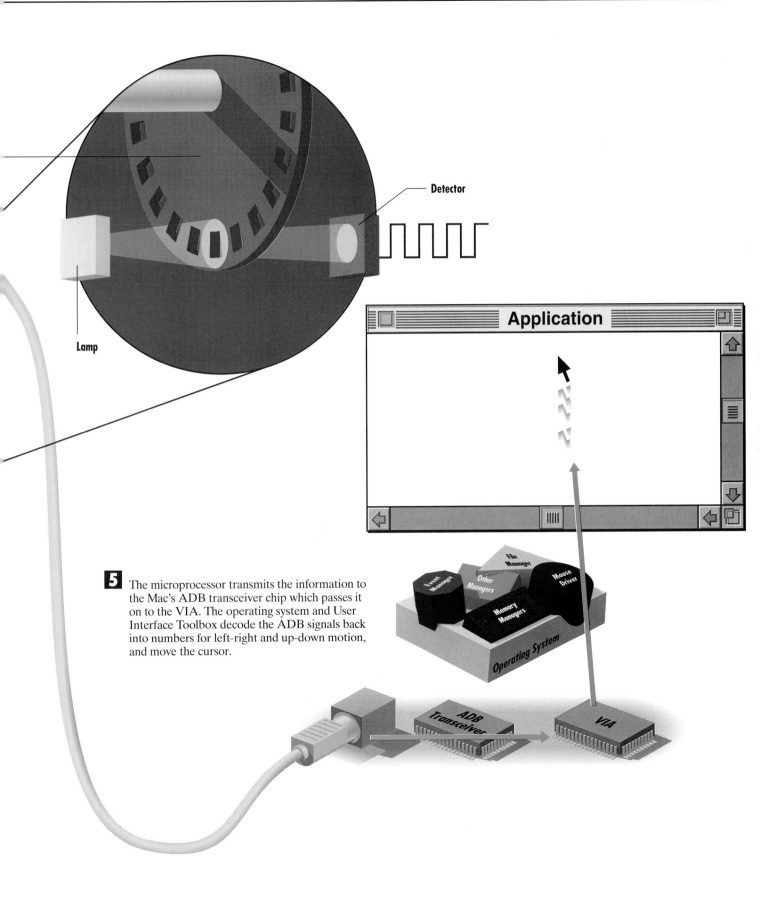

Detector

Lamp

Application

5 The microprocessor transmits the information to the Mac's ADB transceiver chip which passes it on to the VIA. The operating system and User Interface Toolbox decode the ADB signals back into numbers for left-right and up-down motion, and move the cursor.

File Manager

Event Manager

Other Managers

Mouse Driver

Memory Managers

Operating System

ADB Transceiver

VIA

How NuBus Works

ALTHOUGH THE MAC has many functions built onto the logic board (such as circuitry for video and networking), some people need to tailor the Mac to their needs by adding expansion cards. For example, a graphics designer may need a 21-inch monitor card and a graphics accelerator, a stockbroker may need a 486 coprocessor card to run Windows software, and a scientist could collect experimental data with a Mac and an analog-to-digital card. You might even have a need for all these cards. But even if you don't need to add anything to your Mac right now, having expansion slots gives you the ability to expand and upgrade a Mac's capabilities at a later date should you need to.

NuBus is the method for adding one or more expansion cards to Macs that are descended from the Mac II, the first user-configurable Mac, released in 1987. NuBus has been used in most modular Macs, including the Mac IIsi, IIci, and Centris, as well as the Quadra and Duo Dock. Classic-style Macs and LCs don't use NuBus.

NuBus was designed and is patented by Texas Instruments and is specified by an industry standard called IEEE 1196. The specification calls for a 96-pin DIN connector in three rows of 32 pins. Data and address lines, which are separate on the Mac logic board, are combined on NuBus, and they are a full 32 bits wide. NuBus can theoretically handle up to 16 NuBus slots, though Apple has never used more than 6 slots in a Mac. However, you can buy an external expansion chassis for additional slots.

NuBus was designed to be just as easy to use as the rest of the Mac. NuBus cards are self-configuring; plug them into any slot, and they work. Cards are interchangeable from slot to slot and from Mac to Mac without requiring you to change hardware or software settings.

NuBus also gives cards access to the Mac RAM. This is possible because each card has its own ROM that contains the necessary parameters for self-configuration and communications with the rest of the Mac. Cards use routines in the operating system's Slot Manager, located in the Mac's ROM (or in the System file in older Macs). The Slot Manager directs the NuBus cards to the appropriate operating-system routines. Power is supplied to the cards by directing the Mac's power supply through the NuBus slots.

NuBus

1 At startup, the Slot Manager initializes each NuBus card, which prepares them for operation and gives them identification numbers, usually between 9 and 14.

2 The Slot Manager reinitializes the cards after ROM patches (updated operating-system code) are loaded from the System file into RAM. This is in case some of the cards require the ROM patches for certain operations.

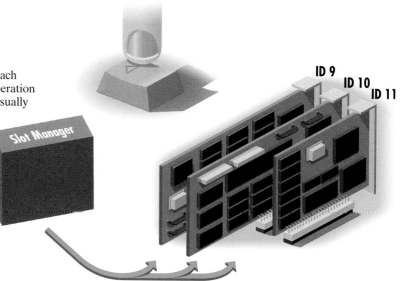
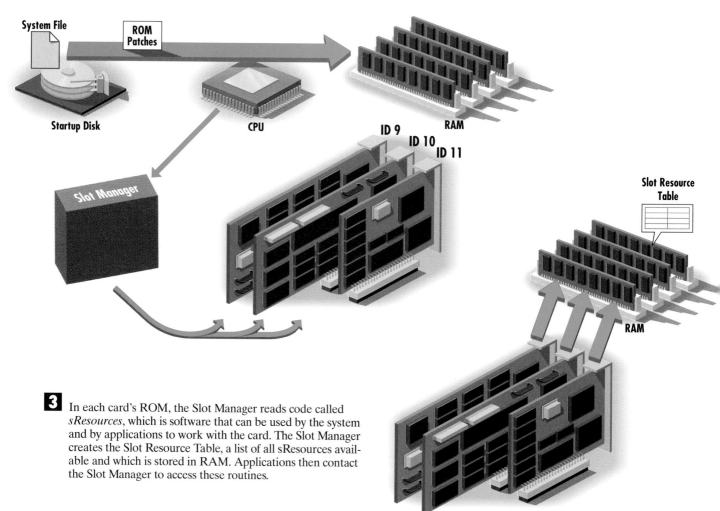

3 In each card's ROM, the Slot Manager reads code called *sResources*, which is software that can be used by the system and by applications to work with the card. The Slot Manager creates the Slot Resource Table, a list of all sResources available and which is stored in RAM. Applications then contact the Slot Manager to access these routines.

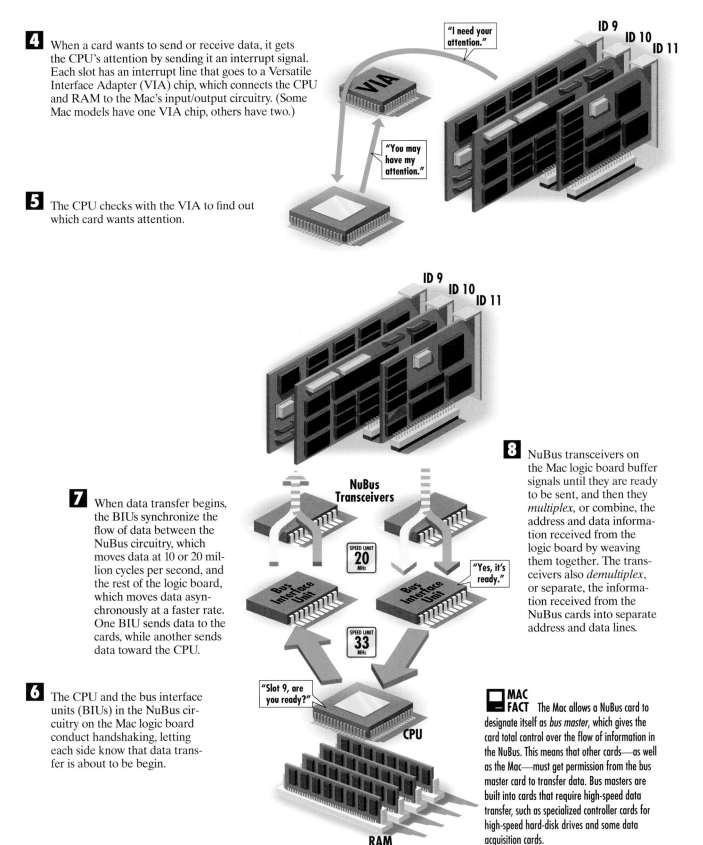

4 When a card wants to send or receive data, it gets the CPU's attention by sending it an interrupt signal. Each slot has an interrupt line that goes to a Versatile Interface Adapter (VIA) chip, which connects the CPU and RAM to the Mac's input/output circuitry. (Some Mac models have one VIA chip, others have two.)

"I need your attention."

ID 9
ID 10
ID 11

"You may have my attention."

5 The CPU checks with the VIA to find out which card wants attention.

ID 9
ID 10
ID 11

8 NuBus transceivers on the Mac logic board buffer signals until they are ready to be sent, and then they *multiplex,* or combine, the address and data information received from the logic board by weaving them together. The transceivers also *demultiplex,* or separate, the information received from the NuBus cards into separate address and data lines.

NuBus Transceivers

7 When data transfer begins, the BIUs synchronize the flow of data between the NuBus circuitry, which moves data at 10 or 20 million cycles per second, and the rest of the logic board, which moves data asynchronously at a faster rate. One BIU sends data to the cards, while another sends data toward the CPU.

SPEED LIMIT **20** MHz

"Yes, it's ready."

Bus Interface Unit

Bus Interface Unit

SPEED LIMIT **33** MHz

6 The CPU and the bus interface units (BIUs) in the NuBus circuitry on the Mac logic board conduct handshaking, letting each side know that data transfer is about to be begin.

"Slot 9, are you ready?"

CPU

RAM

MAC FACT The Mac allows a NuBus card to designate itself as *bus master,* which gives the card total control over the flow of information in the NuBus. This means that other cards—as well as the Mac—must get permission from the bus master card to transfer data. Bus masters are built into cards that require high-speed data transfer, such as specialized controller cards for high-speed hard-disk drives and some data acquisition cards.

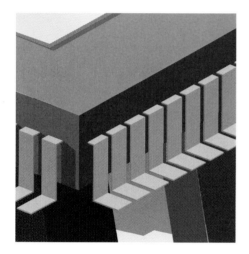

How Processor Direct Slots (PDSs) Work

I F YOUR MAC has a single expansion slot, chances are it's a *processor direct slot*, or *PDS*. Unlike other ports or expansion slots in the Mac, a PDS has a direct line to the central processing unit (CPU), a hot line to the top chip.

The first PDS was designed to be a simple expansion slot in the Mac SE. Since then, every classic-style Mac has had a PDS in one form or another, and several modular Macs sport PDSs as well. Today, the PDS is known as a faster alternative to NuBus and has been included in high-end Macs that also come with NuBus slots, such as the IIfx and Quadra models.

The PDS was not designed as a bus architecture, which means there can only be a single PDS per Mac. However, because it is not a bus, PDS signals aren't slowed down by the types of processing circuitry found in NuBus and SCSI. A PDS is connected directly to the system bus on the logic board, giving an expansion card direct access to the CPU and RAM. Because a PDS is faster than NuBus, accelerator cards are often designed to fit in a Mac's PDS. Other types of cards that perform well in PDSs include network interface cards, RAM disks, and video cards.

The PDS is an odd slot in that it is not standard across all Mac models, as are other input/output systems like NuBus and SCSI. This means that cards developed for one type of PDS won't work on another. A few models do have the same type of PDS; for instance, the Mac LC, LC III, and Color Classic have slots that are compatible with each other. However, these three machines are the exceptions; most Macs with different CPUs (68000, 68030, and 68040) have different PDSs. In addition, Macs that also have NuBus slots use a different PDS than Macs that have only a PDS for expansion.

The number of pins of the PDS varies between different versions, usually from 96 to 120, set in three rows. However, the signals on the pins can be different on PDSs with the same number of pins, making the PDSs incompatible.

Processor Direct Slot (PDS)

Modern Macs, which use either 68030 or 68040 processors, use 64 of the PDS pins for 32-bit data and 32-bit addressing (1 bit per pin). Several pins are used to supply power and ground to the card. The remaining pins are connected to signal lines, which transfer control information.

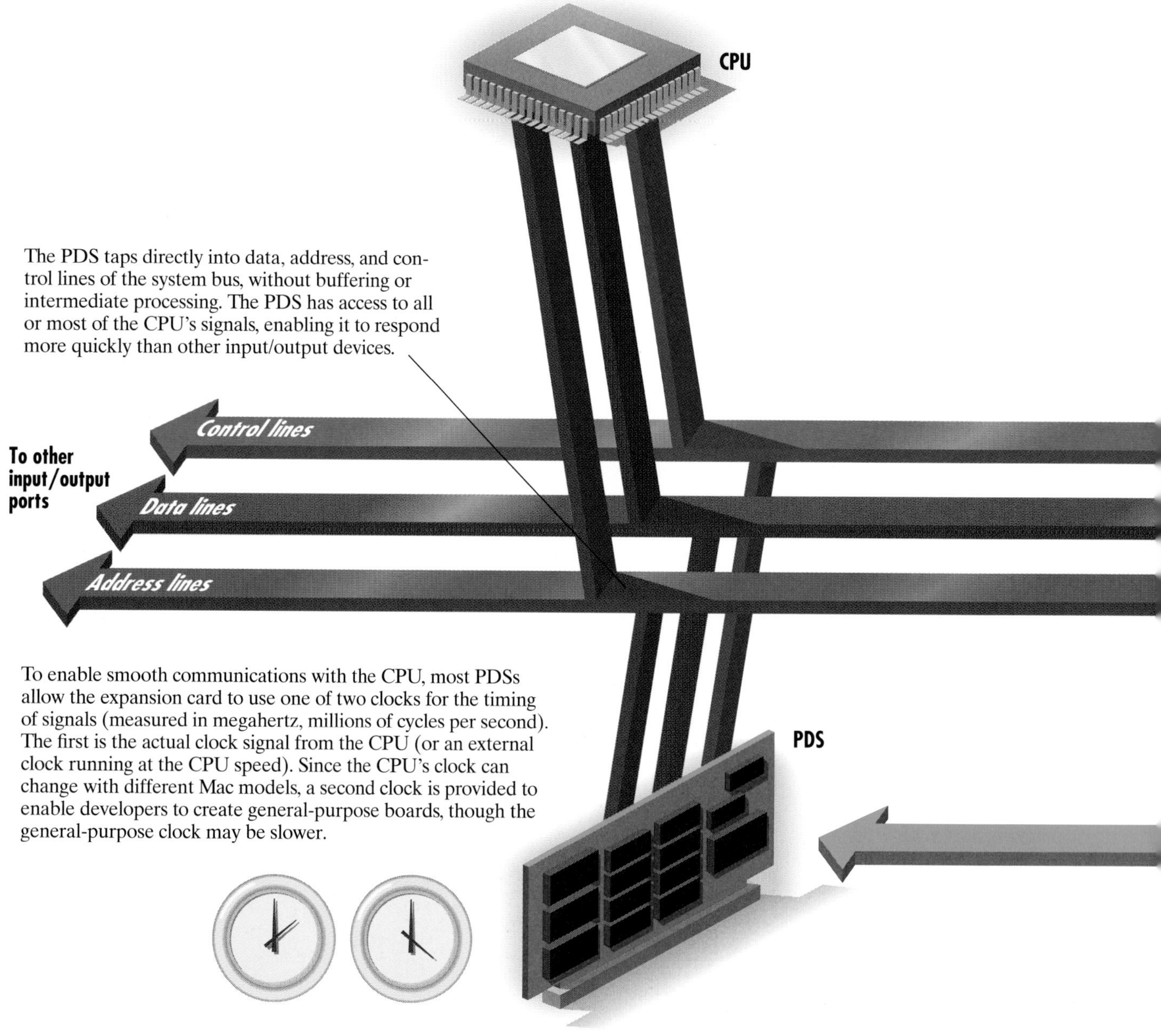

CPU

The PDS taps directly into data, address, and control lines of the system bus, without buffering or intermediate processing. The PDS has access to all or most of the CPU's signals, enabling it to respond more quickly than other input/output devices.

Control lines

To other input/output ports

Data lines

Address lines

To enable smooth communications with the CPU, most PDSs allow the expansion card to use one of two clocks for the timing of signals (measured in megahertz, millions of cycles per second). The first is the actual clock signal from the CPU (or an external clock running at the CPU speed). Since the CPU's clock can change with different Mac models, a second clock is provided to enable developers to create general-purpose boards, though the general-purpose clock may be slower.

PDS

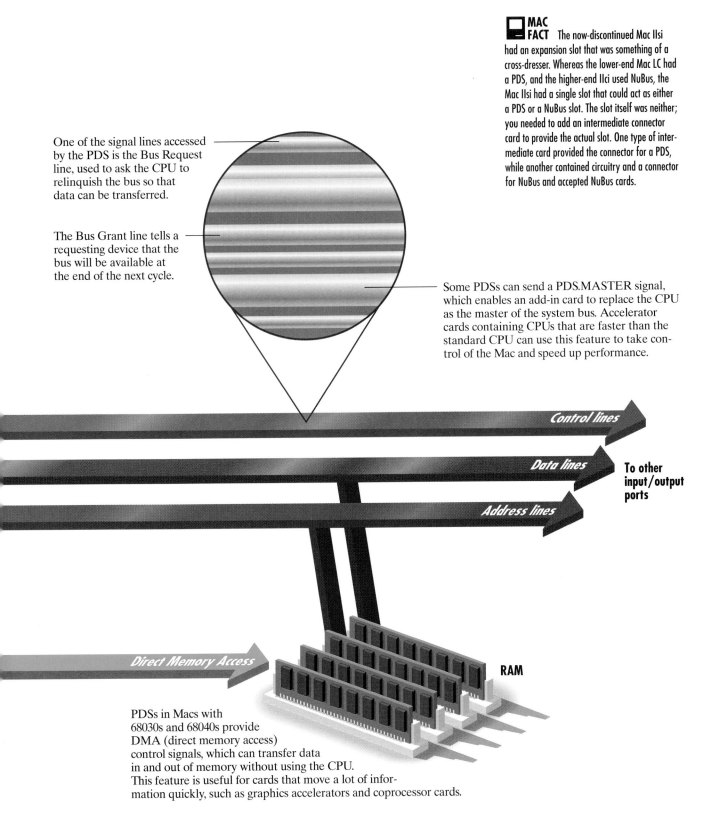

One of the signal lines accessed by the PDS is the Bus Request line, used to ask the CPU to relinquish the bus so that data can be transferred.

The Bus Grant line tells a requesting device that the bus will be available at the end of the next cycle.

Some PDSs can send a PDS.MASTER signal, which enables an add-in card to replace the CPU as the master of the system bus. Accelerator cards containing CPUs that are faster than the standard CPU can use this feature to take control of the Mac and speed up performance.

Control lines

Data lines

To other input/output ports

Address lines

Direct Memory Access

RAM

PDSs in Macs with 68030s and 68040s provide DMA (direct memory access) control signals, which can transfer data in and out of memory without using the CPU. This feature is useful for cards that move a lot of information quickly, such as graphics accelerators and coprocessor cards.

CHAPTER 22

How Serial Ports Work

SINCE BEFORE THE first Mac, computers have used serial ports to add input/output devices. Serial ports transmit data the old-fashioned way, one bit a time. Despite the proliferation of faster communications ports, serial ports are still fast enough to remain a mainstream method of moving data in and out of computers.

The two serial ports in every Mac, the printer and modem ports, enable the Mac to talk to the world outside your office through a modem or a local area network. They can also run desktop devices such as low-end printers and MIDI-capable musical instruments. You can even make a direct connection to another Mac or a PC using serial ports.

The printer and modem ports are almost identical, and most modems, printers, and other devices can be run on either port. Typically, the port you use is set in the software you are using.

Both ports are controlled by the same chip, the Serial Communications Controller (SCC), and follow the RS-422 standard for data transmission. RS-422 is a newer and somewhat better transmission method than the RS-232 serial ports used in IBM-compatible PCs, in that signals can travel for longer distances and are less affected by line noise.

A serial port, usually the printer port, can also be used to connect to LocalTalk local area networks, which gives you access to laser printers and other network communications. In LocalTalk mode, a serial port is taken over by the operating system's AppleTalk Manager, which speeds up the maximum transmission rate by a factor of four. This results in printer performance similar to that of parallel ports on IBM-compatible PCs, but at distances up to about a hundred times greater.

Modem and Printer Ports

The Mac serial ports use miniature 8-pin connectors of a type called mini-DIN. Data is transmitted over two pins, and it is received over another two. Two other pins are used for hand-shaking: one for input and one for output. The remaining pins are used for a ground signal (0 volts) and a general purpose input signal, which is used by some devices.

Parallel

RAM

1 The Serial Communications Controller (SCC) runs both printer and modem ports. For signals leaving the Mac, the SCC chip converts the parallel signals of the logic board to serial signals. For signals entering the Mac, the SCC does a serial-to-parallel conversion.

Serial

CPU

Interrupts

Data

VIA

2 The SCC generates handshaking signals to establish a link with a device such as a modem connected to the serial port. On pin 1, the SCC sends a Data Terminal Ready (DTR) signal required for modem transmission. The modem sends back a Clear to Send (CTS) signal on pin 2.

"Are you ready?"

SCC

6 When applications such as telecommunications or MIDI (musical instrument data interface) music software want to send data through the serial ports, they send commands to the Mac Toolbox, which controls the SCC chip at a maximum data transmission rate of 57,600 bits per second. This is faster than modems can transmit data over telephone lines. The hardware itself can support faster rates, and does, when the operating system's AppleTalk Manager uses a serial port for LocalTalk network transmissions. Most software is programmed to use the printer port for LocalTalk. The AppleTalk Manager runs the SCC chip at 230,400 bits per second for LocalTalk signals.

SPEED LIMIT
57.6
kbps

SPEED LIMIT
230.4
kbps

AppleTalk Manager

Toolbox

Operating System

MAC FACT For most of the time you use your modem port, it is running in asynchronous mode, which requires the Mac and the peripheral to frequently exchange handshaking signals. The modem port also supports synchronous transmission of data, which doesn't use handshaking. In synchronous mode, the modem port can transmit data at a theoretical maximum of 900,000 bits per second, some 15 times faster than normal. Synchronous communications is sometimes used to connect to mainframes, but is not common because it is more difficult than asynchronous transmission to implement in Mac peripherals.

4 Digital data is sent to the modem with an inverted copy of the signal. A binary 1 is represented as a low voltage. Instead of comparing the bit to 0 volts to determine whether it is high or low, RS-422 compares the voltage of the bit with the inverted signal. This results in a large difference between 0 bit and 1 bit, making the signal more immune to line noise. The transmit signal and its inverted signal are sent to the modem on pins 6 and 3; the receive signal is on pins 8 and 5.

3 Chips called drivers do the actual transmitting and receiving of signals. Radio-frequency interference (RFI) filters clean up incoming and outgoing signals.

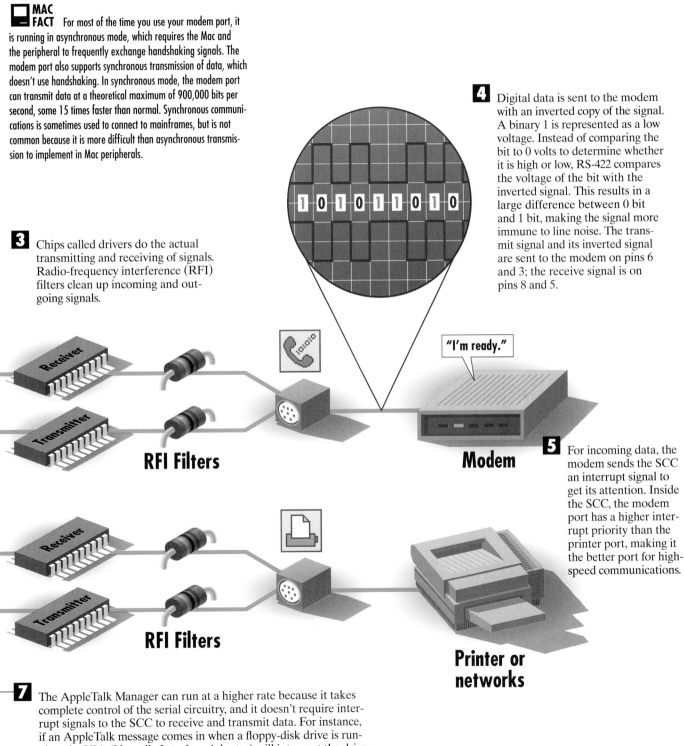

RFI Filters

Modem

"I'm ready."

5 For incoming data, the modem sends the SCC an interrupt signal to get its attention. Inside the SCC, the modem port has a higher interrupt priority than the printer port, making it the better port for high-speed communications.

RFI Filters

Printer or networks

7 The AppleTalk Manager can run at a higher rate because it takes complete control of the serial circuitry, and it doesn't require interrupt signals to the SCC to receive and transmit data. For instance, if an AppleTalk message comes in when a floppy-disk drive is running, the VIA (Versatile Interface Adapter) will interrupt the drive to send data to the CPU or RAM. You may also notice a slowdown in an application when a network file transfer is occurring in the background.

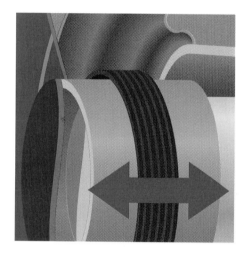

CHAPTER
23

How Sound Works

ONE OF THE innovative things about the Mac has always been its ability to use sound to tell you things. Beeps and quacks tell you when you've done something wrong or right, and voices and music add depth to presentations. Built-in sound also enables you to use an off-the-shelf Mac to play, import, or create music.

Every Mac has a speaker and a sound output port that you can use to connect external speakers or standard audio recording devices. Many of the more recent Macs sport sound input ports and plug-in or built-in microphones, as well. Sampled sounds can be added electronically as disk files, enabling Macs to sound like the Starship *Enterprise* or an orchestra playing Mahler symphonies.

Another way to input and output sound is through the serial ports in the form of MIDI (musical instrument data interface) signals. MIDI enables Mac software to control and record music from electronic musical instruments such as keyboards and synthesizers. It is not uncommon to see Macs on stage with musicians.

MIDI signals differ from the signals moving through the sound ports in one major way. Like most of the Mac's input/output signals, MIDI data consists of digital streams of 1s and 0s. Signals moving through the sound ports, however, are analog, like the signals that come out of your home stereo. Analog signals consist of constantly fluctuating voltages of varying strength (amplitude) and rapidity (frequency).

The Mac can play several types of sound in stereo or mono. It can create simple sounds, such as alert sounds, or more complex sounds, such as a synthetic voice. The Mac can also play back complex sampled sounds that have been recorded by the Mac through a sound input port, moved to the Mac as a file, or imported from an external MIDI device. Newer Macs can mix and synchronize multiple sounds, as well as play sounds from a disk while other tasks are being executed.

You can record your own sounds for use as system alerts or for use in applications as audio notes or entertainment. For Macs with sound input ports or built-in microphones, you can use the Sound control panel or a third-party application to start and stop recording. There are even applications that turn voice input into system commands. So if you see someone talking to a Mac, he or she is not necessarily crazy.

Playing Sound

Sounds on the Mac can be stored as resources in the System Folder (like fonts) or as sound files, which specify the sound commands and synthesizer routines to be used. The simplest sounds, such as the system alerts you can select in the Sound control panel, are stored as snd resources. More complex sounds can be stored as syth resources. Most sounds can be stored as AIFF (audio interchange file format) files, which can be easily shared by different applications.

2 The Sound Manager calls up sound commands (instructions to play or modify a sound) from ROM and either creates or calls up (depending on what the application needs) one or more *sound channels*, which are queues of sound commands required to produce a sound. The Sound Manager can create and run multiple sound channels at the same time. For instance, the system can play an alert beep (to tell you that you are having a printing problem, for instance) at the same time an application is playing music for a multimedia presentation. Multiple sound channels can also be mixed to combine voice and music or multiple tracks of music.

1 When an application needs to play a sound, it sends commands to the operating system's Sound Manager. The application can specify exactly what to do or it can reference a resource or a sound file that contains the sound commands and sound synthesizer.

3 The Sound Manager calls up code resources called *synthesizers* to interpret the sound commands in the sound channels and to direct the sound chips to produce the sounds. The synthesizer takes control of the Apple Sound Chip on the logic board and loads digital samples into the chip's buffers. There are several types of synthesizers stored in the System file: A square wave synthesizer generates simple sounds, a wave table synthesizer creates more complex sounds, and a sampled sound synthesizer plays digitally recorded sounds.

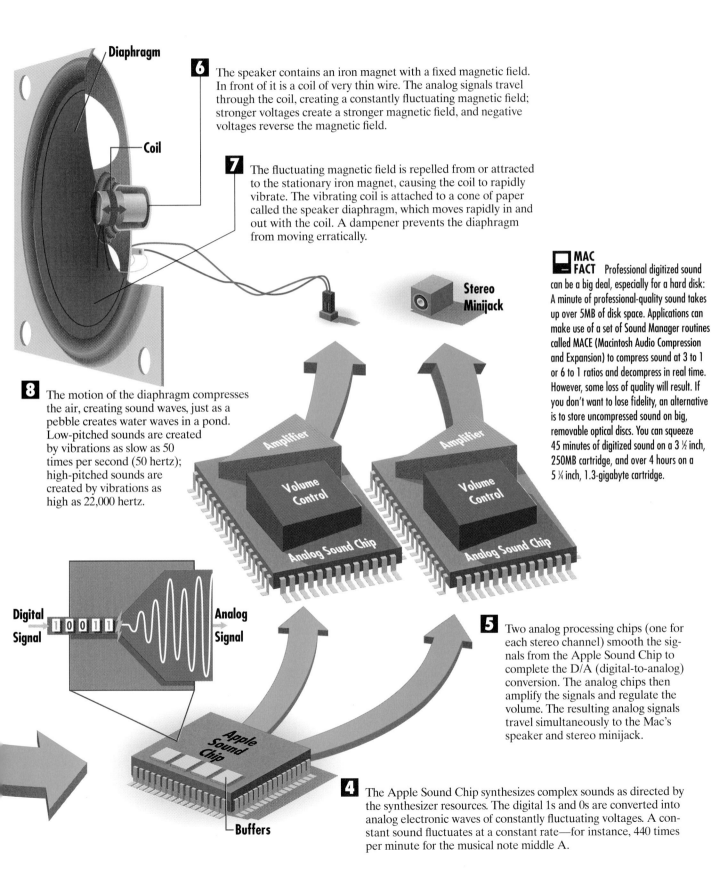

Diaphragm

Coil

6 The speaker contains an iron magnet with a fixed magnetic field. In front of it is a coil of very thin wire. The analog signals travel through the coil, creating a constantly fluctuating magnetic field; stronger voltages create a stronger magnetic field, and negative voltages reverse the magnetic field.

7 The fluctuating magnetic field is repelled from or attracted to the stationary iron magnet, causing the coil to rapidly vibrate. The vibrating coil is attached to a cone of paper called the speaker diaphragm, which moves rapidly in and out with the coil. A dampener prevents the diaphragm from moving erratically.

Stereo Minijack

MAC FACT Professional digitized sound can be a big deal, especially for a hard disk: A minute of professional-quality sound takes up over 5MB of disk space. Applications can make use of a set of Sound Manager routines called MACE (Macintosh Audio Compression and Expansion) to compress sound at 3 to 1 or 6 to 1 ratios and decompress in real time. However, some loss of quality will result. If you don't want to lose fidelity, an alternative is to store uncompressed sound on big, removable optical discs. You can squeeze 45 minutes of digitized sound on a 3 ½ inch, 250MB cartridge, and over 4 hours on a 5 ¼ inch, 1.3-gigabyte cartridge.

8 The motion of the diaphragm compresses the air, creating sound waves, just as a pebble creates water waves in a pond. Low-pitched sounds are created by vibrations as slow as 50 times per second (50 hertz); high-pitched sounds are created by vibrations as high as 22,000 hertz.

Amplifier

Volume Control

Analog Sound Chip

Amplifier

Volume Control

Analog Sound Chip

Digital Signal

1 0 0 1 1

Analog Signal

5 Two analog processing chips (one for each stereo channel) smooth the signals from the Apple Sound Chip to complete the D/A (digital-to-analog) conversion. The analog chips then amplify the signals and regulate the volume. The resulting analog signals travel simultaneously to the Mac's speaker and stereo minijack.

Apple Sound Chip

Buffers

4 The Apple Sound Chip synthesizes complex sounds as directed by the synthesizer resources. The digital 1s and 0s are converted into analog electronic waves of constantly fluctuating voltages. A constant sound fluctuates at a constant rate—for instance, 440 times per minute for the musical note middle A.

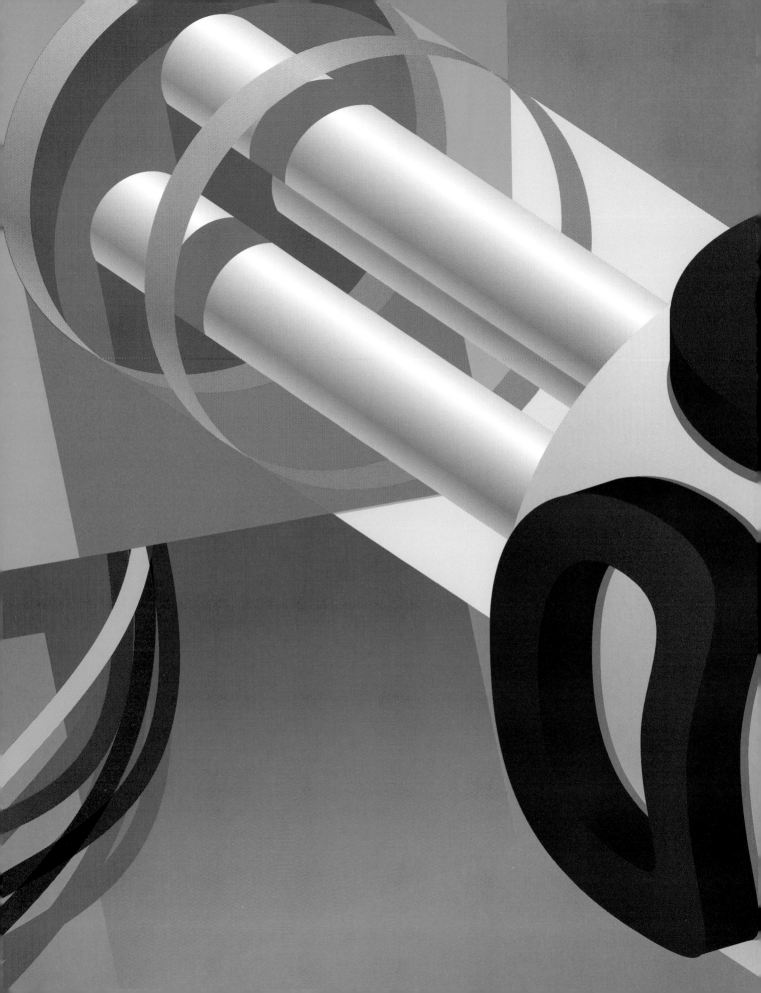

6
DISPLAY

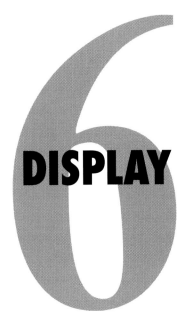

CONTENTS

Active Matrix LCD Display

Flat-panel displays make use of two rather odd properties of physics: the polarization of light, a phenomenon used in sunglasses to partially block out light; and the interaction of light with liquid crystal, a liquid material that shows some properties of solid crystals.

Light Source Polarizing Filter Column Electrode Row Electrode Transistor Top Electrode Variable Electrode

1 The backlighting panel produces white light at the back of the display. Light consists of electromagnetic waves that vibrate in a single plane. White light produces many light waves, which vibrate in every different direction. White light also contains light of every color.

2 The light passes through a *polarizing filter*—a material with embedded crystals—which acts like a grating, allowing only light vibrating in approximately one direction to pass.

3 Thin wires (column and row electrodes) deliver the video signals to thin-film transistors, one for each pixel for monochrome and gray-scale screens, three for each pixel for color displays. In monochrome screens, the transistors are either on or off. However, with gray-scale and color displays, the transistor puts out several levels of current, which will eventually represent different levels of gray or color.

4 Each pixel contains a cell filled with liquid crystal. The transistor drives a transparent variable electrode on one face of the liquid crystal cell, applying a voltage to it.

5 Molecules within the liquid crystal have a fixed orientation with respect to one another. When an electric voltage is applied to the transparent electrode, the orientation of the molecules begins to twist through the cell. Different voltages twist the molecules to different degrees.

6 The twisting of the molecules affects the light passing through the liquid crystal material, rotating the plane of vibration of the light waves.

7 In color displays, the three rays of light for each pixel each pass through a color filter, which is either red, green, or blue. Filters block all colors except one.

8 A second polarizing filter blocks light that is not vibrating in a plane aligned with the filter. Light that was rotated through a liquid crystal cell with a full voltage applied passes completely through. Light that passed through a cell with no charge and was therefore not rotated is completely blocked. Light that was rotated partially will be partially passed, providing a lesser amount of red, green, or blue (or gray if gray scale). As with a cathode-ray tube monitor, the three colors in close proximity appear to the eye to blend to form another color.

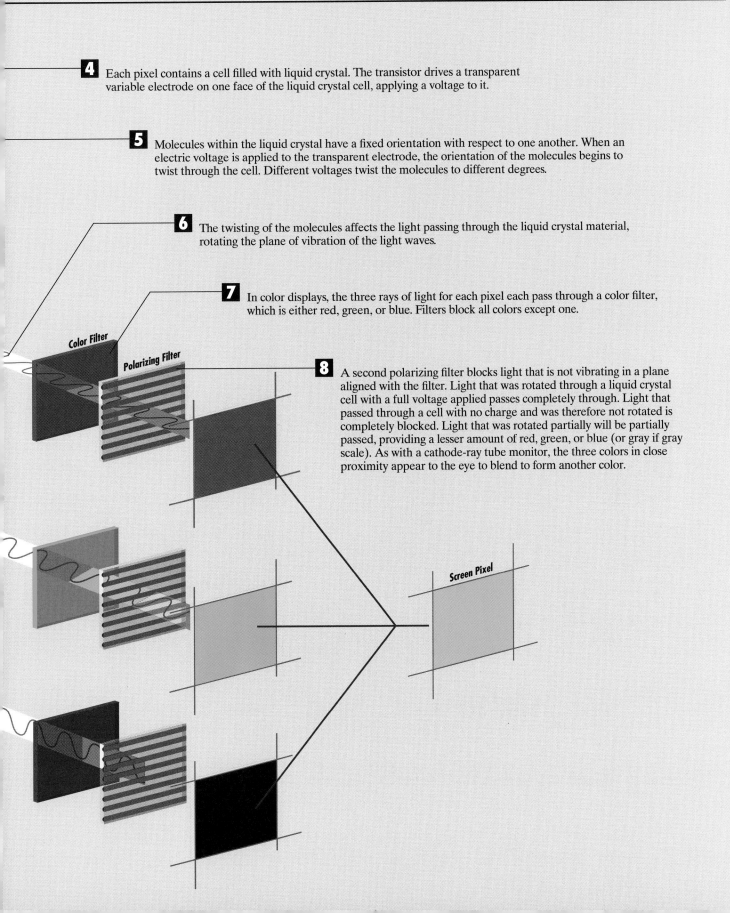

Color Filter

Polarizing Filter

Screen Pixel

Passive Matrix LCDs

Passive matrix LCDs are simpler than active matrix, but work similarly. Instead of being controlled by a transistor, the voltage for each pixel is controlled from the logic board's video circuitry. Shown here is a monochrome display, which has only two voltages and therefore two levels of light twisting: on and off, which produce black and white.

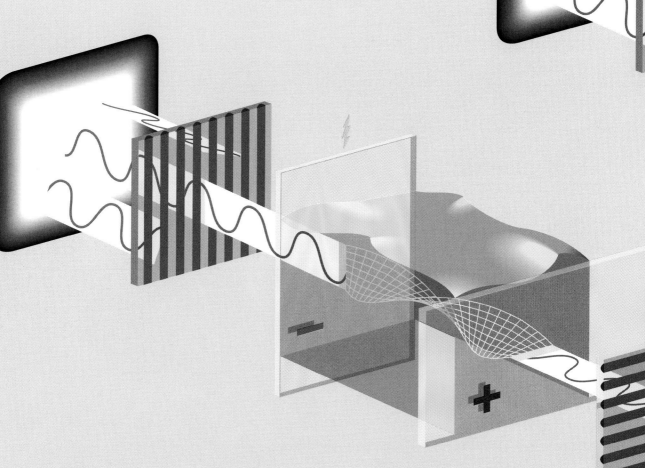

Light Source

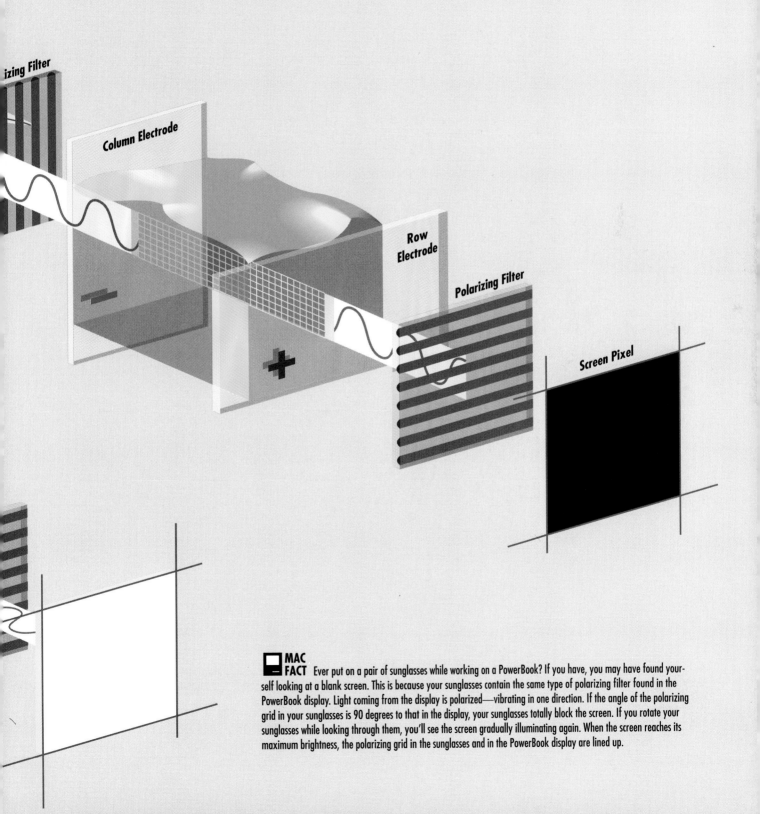

izing Filter

Column Electrode

Row Electrode

Polarizing Filter

Screen Pixel

MAC FACT Ever put on a pair of sunglasses while working on a PowerBook? If you have, you may have found yourself looking at a blank screen. This is because your sunglasses contain the same type of polarizing filter found in the PowerBook display. Light coming from the display is polarized—vibrating in one direction. If the angle of the polarizing grid in your sunglasses is 90 degrees to that in the display, your sunglasses totally block the screen. If you rotate your sunglasses while looking through them, you'll see the screen gradually illuminating again. When the screen reaches its maximum brightness, the polarizing grid in the sunglasses and in the PowerBook display are lined up.

NETWORKS

WITH COMPUTER TECHNOLOGY being such a precise field, it is surprising how ambiguously the term *computer network* is used. Sometimes it's used to describe the type of cable connecting network devices, and other times it's used to describe the hardware circuits generating signals to run over the cable. A network may also be described in terms of the protocols that enable different devices to understand one another. Actually, a network is a system containing all these things, as well as computers, printers, servers, and other devices acting together to improve the usefulness of all the devices.

Networks bring to your Mac the benefits of shared resources. For instance, electronic mail and file servers enable you to send messages and files to people when they aren't at their desks, and electronic calendars let you set up meetings and appointments with people you haven't seen for weeks. These and other network resources, called network services, are applications running on dedicated machines called servers. Servers can be Macs, PCs, or mainframe computers.

AppleTalk is the networking system built into Macs and most network printers. In fact, AppleTalk began as a method of sharing laser printers among multiple Mac users. Prior to the LaserWriter, a shared printer had to be directly connected to an individual computer on a network or to a central control box, which was connected to personal computers via slow serial links. Making a printer an independent network device gave it the flexibility to be located anywhere, with communciations speeds several times faster than with serial connections.

The network originally designed for printers can now connect Macs to computers and networks all over the world. Gateways can connect AppleTalk networks to networks running other types of protocols, such as TCP/IP (Transmission Control Protocol/Internet Protocol), which is popular in government, academic, and large corporate network circles. Macs can also be put directly on networks running TCP/IP and the IPX (Internetwork Packet Exchange) protocol used in Novell NetWare networks, which are popular at sites with PCs. These connections give Mac users access to services running on PCs, UNIX machines, and mainframe computers.

Installing a small AppleTalk network is as easy as connecting a printer to your Mac. Anyone can create a small network using twisted pair cables and inexpensive connectors. Built into every Mac are the hardware and software that create and receive network signals, the Chooser utility to access printers and file servers, and System 7's file-sharing feature, which lets other network users access designated files and folders on your hard disk.

From these simple beginnings, AppleTalk networks can be upgraded to include hundreds of Macs, PCs, printers, and dedicated file, mail, and database servers. Bigger networks require special network devices such as hubs and routers to control the data running over the cables. AppleTalk network data can travel over several types of wire cables, as well as over optical cables for high-quality, ultrasecure networks. The use of wireless networks, which transmit data through the air using infrared or radio waves, is gaining momentum as the technology improves.

CHAPTER

How AppleTalk Works

APPLETALK IS AS intrinsic a part of the Mac as any of the other input/output systems, and it is designed to be as easy to set up and use. Installing a small AppleTalk network is a simple matter of plugging in some cabling between Macs and printers. However, AppleTalk can also be used on networks of thousands of Macs and PCs. AppleTalk is a versatile network, running on a variety of cabling schemes and network interface hardware, and it can be used over telephone links and across nationwide networks.

Everything you need to set up an AppleTalk network is built into the Mac: the hardware that creates the signals, the protocols that enable communications, and the software to enable you to print and share files. You can also add hardware and software to enhance the speed and features of AppleTalk and provide more and faster services.

The AppleTalk Manager in the Mac's ROM provides each Mac with a set of *network protocols*, rules that enable each device to speak the same language when communicating over the network. The AppleTalk Manager also drives the Mac-to-network interface hardware. LocalTalk, the original AppleTalk network interface, is built into every Mac and into most network printers you can buy. LocalTalk is the easiest and least expensive method of transmitting AppleTalk.

AppleTalk is not limited to LocalTalk, and some Macs also come with built-in Ethernet, a faster method of communications. Ethernet operates at a maximum of 10 mbps (megabits per second), and LocalTalk operates at 230.4 kbps (kilobits per second); Ethernet add-in cards can be added to Macs that don't have it built in. AppleTalk also runs on less common network interface hardware, such as token ring, FDDI, and ARCnet. PCs running DOS, Windows, or UNIX can also be added to AppleTalk networks to share the resources of the network and communicate with Macs.

The Mac's software for accessing network services begins with printer access and the queuing of print jobs (also called spooling). The Print Monitor utility provided print spooling for years, but QuickDraw GX (introduced in 1993 for System 7.1 or later) adds Desktop Printers, which are icons representing printers that allow printing of files and moving of print jobs between printers using drag-and-drop techniques.

System 7's file sharing enables you to pass files between Macs and PCs that have software that is compatible with the AppleTalk Filing Protocol (AFP). AFP provides Mac users with a consistent interface, so that networked hard disks appear on the desktop as volumes, much as hard disks connected to the Mac on your desk do. Shared hard disks or folders from other users appear the same as hard disks on file servers such as AppleShare or AFP-compatible servers running on PCs. To the user, AFP servers running on a Mac, PC, UNIX machine, or VAX all look and act the same.

Mac users have been able to use electronic mail for a long time, but the Apple Open Collaboration Environment (introduced in 1993 for System 7.1 or later) lets you send or read electronic mail from almost anywhere in the Mac, whether you are in an application or in the Finder.

AppleTalk Addressing

All networks deliver messages the way a messenger service delivers packages, using addresses that consist of a node number and a network number. AppleTalk is a self-configuring network, in that the Macs create their own node numbers every time they start up or join a network. Users never see the node number, but use English names to identify Macs on an AppleTalk network.

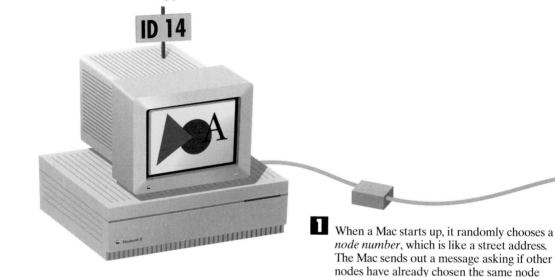

1 When a Mac starts up, it randomly chooses a *node number*, which is like a street address. The Mac sends out a message asking if other nodes have already chosen the same node number.

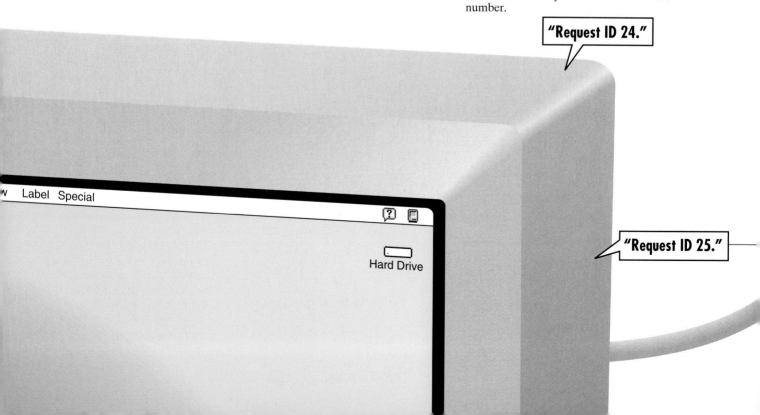

"Request ID 24."

"Request ID 25."

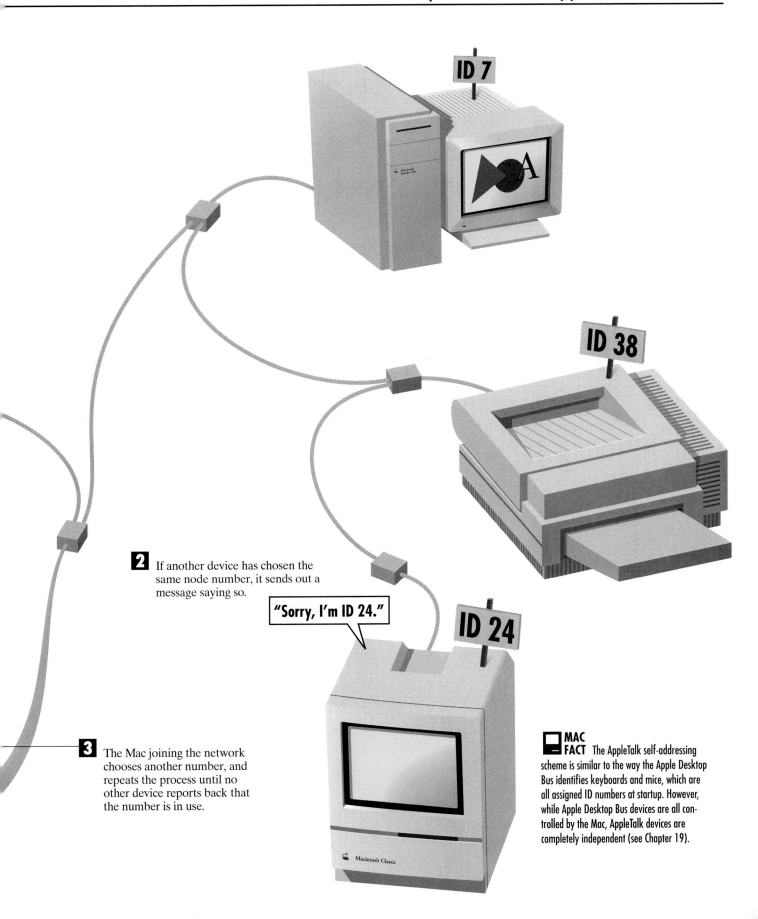

ID 7

ID 38

2 If another device has chosen the same node number, it sends out a message saying so.

"Sorry, I'm ID 24."

ID 24

3 The Mac joining the network chooses another number, and repeats the process until no other device reports back that the number is in use.

MAC FACT The AppleTalk self-addressing scheme is similar to the way the Apple Desktop Bus identifies keyboards and mice, which are all assigned ID numbers at startup. However, while Apple Desktop Bus devices are all controlled by the Mac, AppleTalk devices are completely independent (see Chapter 19).

Macintosh Classic

Sending Data over an AppleTalk Network

1 When you make contact with another device on the network—by sending a message or asking for a file on another computer, accessing a database, or using other types of network applications—the application you are using makes calls to the AppleTalk Manager. The AppleTalk Manager provides all the AppleTalk protocols, the rules by which the computers operate. It uses the protocols to send messages through the network hardware.

2 The AppleTalk Manager checks to see which data-link software has been chosen by the user in the Network control panel. You can select the LocalTalk data link to use the Mac's built-in LocalTalk hardware, or you can select the EtherTalk data link for built-in or add-in Ethernet hardware. You can also choose the TokenTalk data link for token-ring hardware, as well as other data links you might have installed. However, all devices on a network must use the same data link.

3 The network interface hardware, either built-in or on an add-in card, sends and receives data over the network in small chunks called *packets* (sometimes referred to as frames). All Macs have LocalTalk (which uses the printer port), and some models have built-in Ethernet hardware as well.

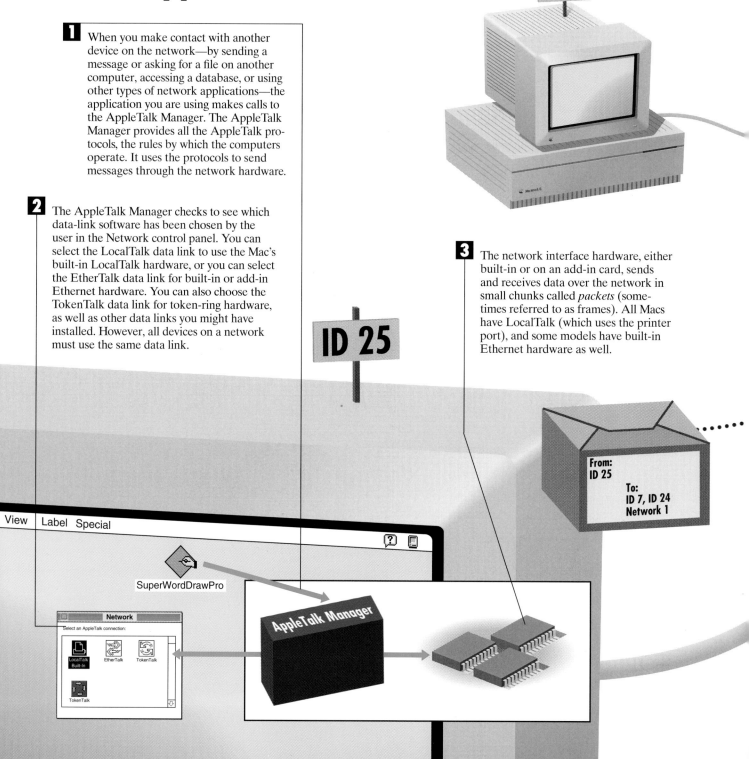

ID 14

ID 25

From:
ID 25

To:
ID 7, ID 24
Network 1

View   Label   Special

SuperWordDrawPro

Network
Select an AppleTalk connection:

LocalTalk
Built-In   EtherTalk   TokenTalk

TokenTalk

AppleTalk Manager

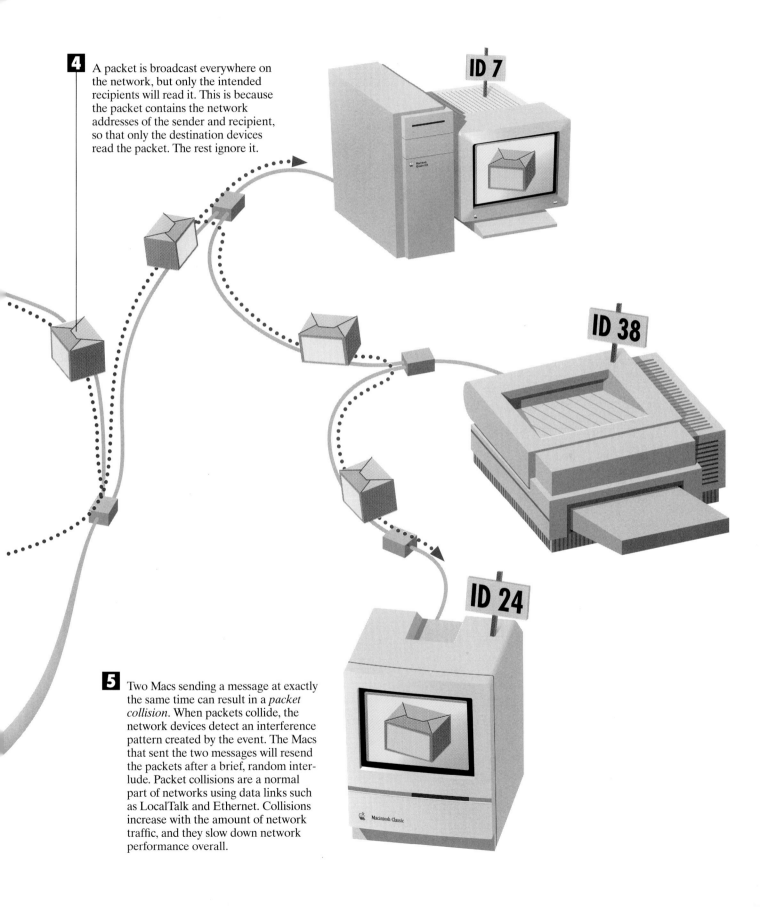

4 A packet is broadcast everywhere on the network, but only the intended recipients will read it. This is because the packet contains the network addresses of the sender and recipient, so that only the destination devices read the packet. The rest ignore it.

ID 7

ID 38

ID 24

5 Two Macs sending a message at exactly the same time can result in a *packet collision*. When packets collide, the network devices detect an interference pattern created by the event. The Macs that sent the two messages will resend the packets after a brief, random interlude. Packet collisions are a normal part of networks using data links such as LocalTalk and Ethernet. Collisions increase with the amount of network traffic, and they slow down network performance overall.

AppleTalk Network Hardware

Small networks of a few Macs don't require anything other than cables and inexpensive connector boxes. When networks grow, several types of equipment are required to keep the network running. One of the most important is a router, which connects two or more networks together to form an internet, or divides a network into two network segments. To each segment, a network administrator must assign a network number, which is sort of like a postal zip code; the network number enables the delivery of messages to the proper network segment.

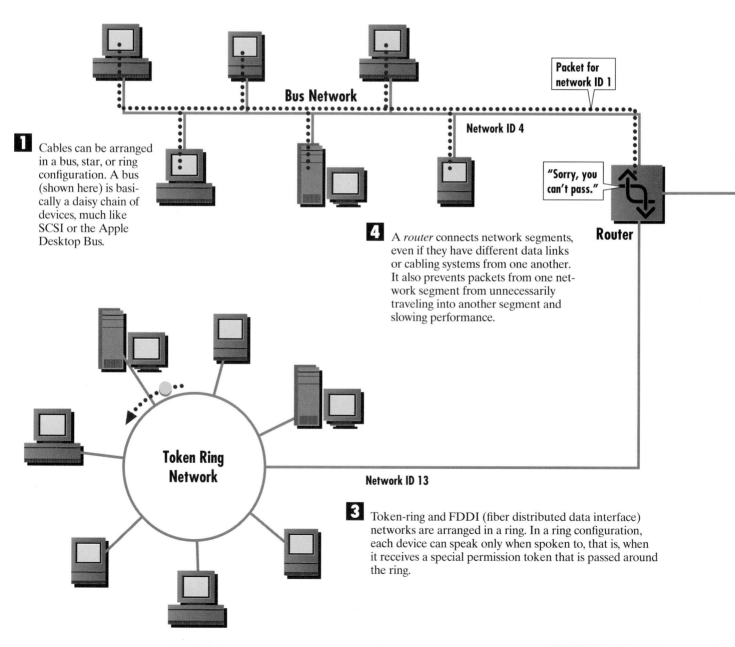

Bus Network

Packet for network ID 1

Network ID 4

"Sorry, you can't pass."

Router

1 Cables can be arranged in a bus, star, or ring configuration. A bus (shown here) is basically a daisy chain of devices, much like SCSI or the Apple Desktop Bus.

4 A *router* connects network segments, even if they have different data links or cabling systems from one another. It also prevents packets from one network segment from unnecessarily traveling into another segment and slowing performance.

Token Ring Network

Network ID 13

3 Token-ring and FDDI (fiber distributed data interface) networks are arranged in a ring. In a ring configuration, each device can speak only when spoken to, that is, when it receives a special permission token that is passed around the ring.

2 A star configuration requires a star hub, a device that receives an incoming packet, boosts the signal, and rebroadcasts the packet to the other network devices. Star hubs enable you to use a total length of cable on the network that is longer than is possible on an unboosted bus. LocalTalk and Ethernet networks can be arranged in star or bus configurations.

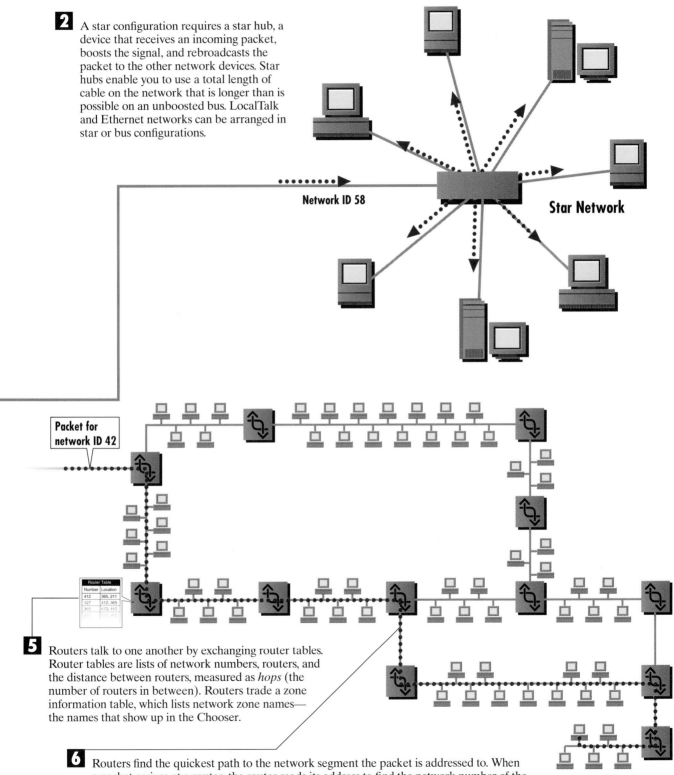

Network ID 58

Star Network

Packet for network ID 42

Router Table

Number	Location
412	365, 211
127	412, 365
365	673, 412

5 Routers talk to one another by exchanging router tables. Router tables are lists of network numbers, routers, and the distance between routers, measured as *hops* (the number of routers in between). Routers trade a zone information table, which lists network zone names—the names that show up in the Chooser.

6 Routers find the quickest path to the network segment the packet is addressed to. When a packet arrives at a router, the router reads its address to find the network number of the packet's destination. The router looks at its routing table to find the path with the fewest hops. The router sends the packet on its way to the next router along the shortest route.

Network ID 42

How the Chooser Works

WHEN APPLE INTRODUCED the LaserWriter in 1985, it needed an easy way for you to choose from among a printer connected directly to your Mac and the multiple laser printers available on an AppleTalk network. The result was Choose Printer, a simple utility in the Apple Menu that eventually became the familiar Chooser, a standard part of Mac system software ever since. Pick the printer type and the specific printer you want to print to, and you're set until you need to change printers. However, the Chooser of today is more than a list of printers. It's a view into an AppleTalk network, enabling you to make connections to network devices such as printers, file servers, shared folders on users' Macs, and, sometimes, other network services.

The Chooser is the place you turn AppleTalk on and off. With AppleTalk turned off, there are two fields, the device-driver field on the upper-left side of the Chooser window and the device field on the upper-right side. Select a device driver and the Chooser gives a list of devices of that type on the right. Turn AppleTalk on and a third field appears on the lower-left side of the screen, listing AppleTalk network zones, which are sections of the network.

The device drivers are also called Chooser extensions (or Rdev files before System 7). There is one Chooser extension for each type of printer: laser printer (LaserWriter), dot-matrix printer (ImageWriter), ink-jet printer (StyleWriter), and so on. The vast majority of network laser printers— over 80 percent—use the LaserWriter driver, though some high-end or color printers use their own drivers. There is a single Chooser extension—the AppleShare driver—for file servers and shared folders.

The Chooser has been around a long time, but it has competition from a new method of connecting to network services. The Apple Open Collaboration Environment (AOCE) provides a special icon on the desktop called the Catalog icon, from which you can choose printers and all other network devices and services. The Catalog icon looks and acts like a folder in the Finder—double-click on it, and you'll see folders containing network and nonnetwork services, including printers, file servers, and fax machines. It can also include services of any non-AppleTalk networks you may be connected to. Users of System 7.1 or later can add AOCE to their Macs, but eventually AOCE will become a standard part of all Mac system software. The AOCE Catalog icon may even replace the Chooser at some point in the future.

The Chooser

MAC FACT To prevent unnecessary network traffic, it's best to close the Chooser when you're not using it. When the Chooser is open, it continues to send out packets every ten seconds or so to update its zone and device lists. Unfortunately, this traffic can contribute to congestion on busy networks. PowerBook users can get extra battery life by turning AppleTalk off. AppleTalk prevents the PowerBook from going into rest mode, a state (invisible to the user) that slows the PowerBook's processing when you're not using it.

1 When the Chooser is opened, it reads the Chooser extension files in the System Folder. The data in these files tell the Chooser what to display when you click on an icon in the device-driver field and when you choose a device.

2 If AppleTalk is *active* (turned on), the Chooser sends out packets requesting routers to send zone information packets. AppleTalk zones are logical groupings of network devices. Zones can contain all devices in a network segment, or they can contain devices in different network segments that are related functionally. For instance, you could set up a zone consisting of the Macs of managers. Zones are created by the network manager when setting up the routers.

3 The Chooser reads the zone information packets that are sent and displays a list of zones. If no zones are detected, it does not display the zone field.

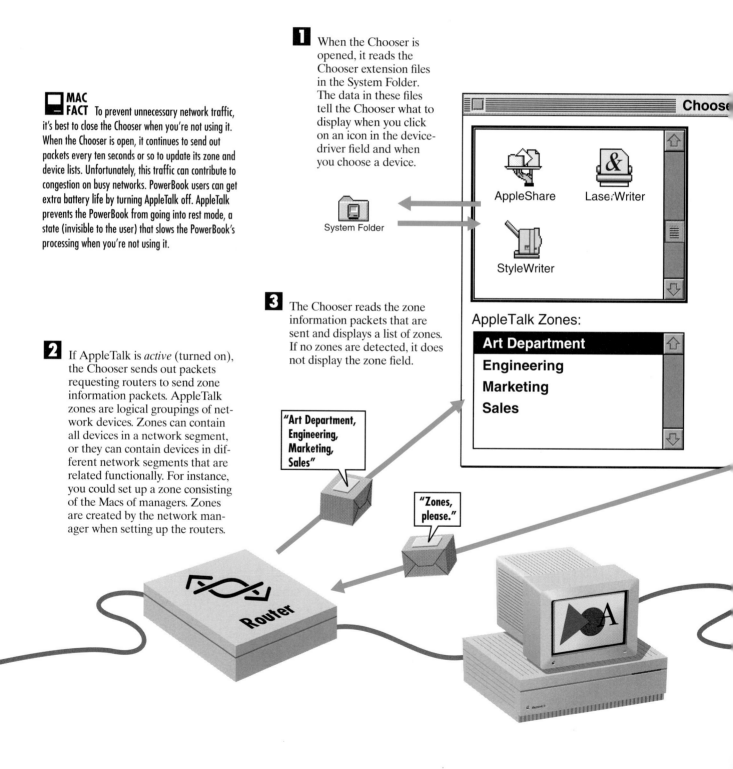

System Folder

Choose

AppleShare   Laser Writer

StyleWriter

AppleTalk Zones:

Art Department
Engineering
Marketing
Sales

"Art Department, Engineering, Marketing, Sales"

"Zones, please."

Router

5 The file servers that show up in the device field are any devices using the AppleTalk Filing Protocol (AFP). This includes AppleShare file servers, Macs using System 7's file sharing, or AFP-compatible servers running on PCs or UNIX machines.

6 When you double-click on a particular file server, the Chooser presents you with a list of volumes (including hard disk drives and shared folders) connected to that machine. Double-clicking on the volume name opens a link between your Mac and the volume and mounts an icon for the volume on your desktop.

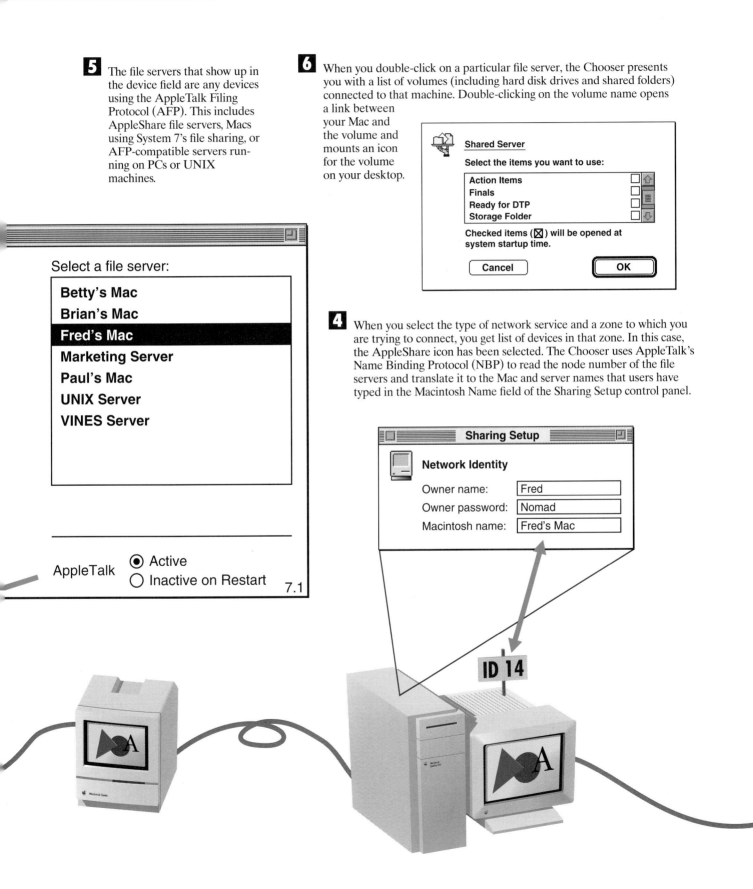

Shared Server

Select the items you want to use:

- Action Items
- Finals
- Ready for DTP
- Storage Folder

Checked items (⊠) will be opened at system startup time.

Cancel   OK

Select a file server:

Betty's Mac
Brian's Mac
Fred's Mac
Marketing Server
Paul's Mac
UNIX Server
VINES Server

AppleTalk   ● Active
             ○ Inactive on Restart   7.1

4 When you select the type of network service and a zone to which you are trying to connect, you get list of devices in that zone. In this case, the AppleShare icon has been selected. The Chooser uses AppleTalk's Name Binding Protocol (NBP) to read the node number of the file servers and translate it to the Mac and server names that users have typed in the Macintosh Name field of the Sharing Setup control panel.

Sharing Setup

Network Identity

Owner name: Fred
Owner password: Nomad
Macintosh name: Fred's Mac

ID 14

CHAPTER
29

How Macs in Non-AppleTalk Environments Work

APPLETALK IS THE Mac's native network language, but it is not the only one used by personal computers. Debates over the pros and cons of various network protocols can be as contentious as those over politics and religion. Fortunately, there are a variety of ways to connect Macs to networks that use all sorts of network protocols.

The most common network protocols are TCP/IP, which is found in UNIX environments and large corporate networks, and IPX, which is used in Novell NetWare networks of IBM-compatible PCs. Also found in PC environments are networks based on variations of NetBIOS, an old PC protocol. Other network protocols in use include SNA (Systems Network Architecture), used with IBM mainframes; OSI (Open Systems Interconnect), popular in large European networks; and DECnet, used with midrange VAX computers.

There are several strategies for connecting Macs to these networks to access services such as electronic mail, file transfer, or databases. You can enable the Mac to speak the foreign (non-AppleTalk) protocol by adding a simple extension file to the System Folder. You can then use software to access the services of the foreign network. This a simple and inexpensive solution for connecting a few Macs to a big non-AppleTalk network.

For large numbers of Macs and a few servers running on PCs or UNIX computers, many foreign network systems allow you to add AppleTalk to the server. In this case, the Macs use AppleTalk while the PCs or UNIX workstations use another network protocol to access services such as the network file servers (NFS) common in UNIX networks.

There are also devices called gateways that connect whole networks of Macs to foreign networks. Gateways translate between AppleTalk and the foreign network protocols. Gateways are practical with large numbers of Macs and foreign servers.

You may want to contact another a Mac on a distant AppleTalk network by going through a large foreign network. This process, called *encapsulation,* or *tunneling,* enables Mac users on different coasts or continents to keep in touch with each other.

Foreign Protocols

1 Dropping an extension such as Apple's
MacTCP or Novell's MacIPX enables a Mac
to recognize foreign network packets that it
would ordinarily ignore. Macs using these
extensions still have access to standard
AppleTalk networks as well.

2 Special applications that can use foreign protocols
enable Macs to access file servers, electronic mail,
and other services on foreign file servers.

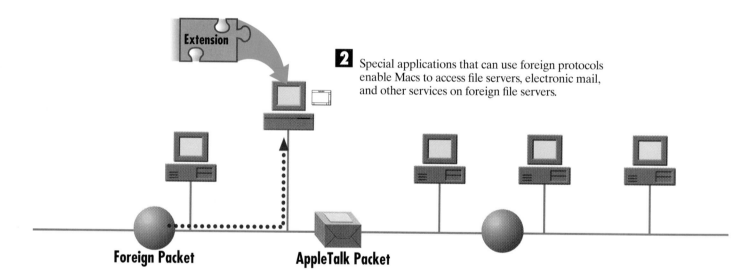

Foreign Packet

AppleTalk Packet

Extension

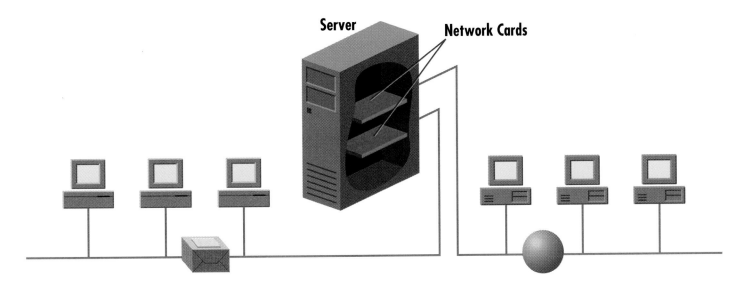

Server   **Network Cards**

3 You can add AppleTalk to many non-Mac network servers, such as Novell NetWare, Banyan VINES, and UNIX-based servers. In this setup, the server communicates with Macs using AppleTalk and with PCs using its native network protocol.

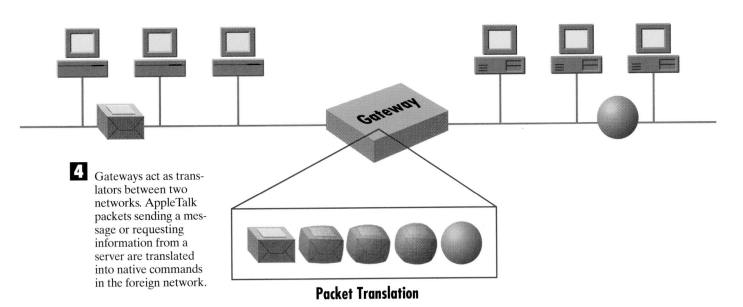

Gateway

4 Gateways act as translators between two networks. AppleTalk packets sending a message or requesting information from a server are translated into native commands in the foreign network.

Packet Translation

Tunneling

Tunneling (also called encapsulation) is a method that lets two AppleTalk networks connected by one or more foreign (non-AppleTalk) networks communicate with each other. The two networks can be in adjacent buildings or on opposite coasts.

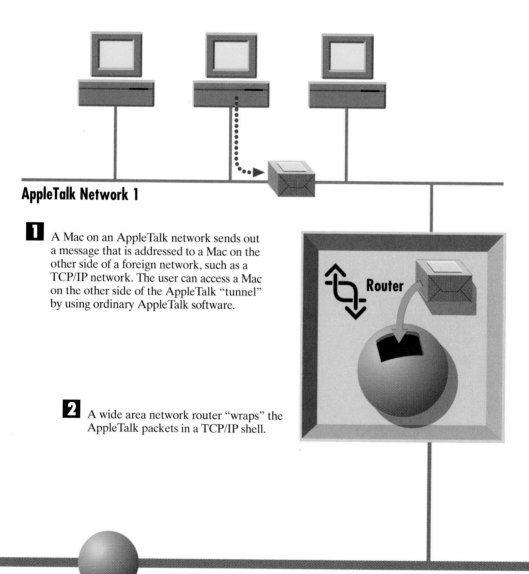

AppleTalk Network 1

1 A Mac on an AppleTalk network sends out a message that is addressed to a Mac on the other side of a foreign network, such as a TCP/IP network. The user can access a Mac on the other side of the AppleTalk "tunnel" by using ordinary AppleTalk software.

Router

2 A wide area network router "wraps" the AppleTalk packets in a TCP/IP shell.

TCP/IP Network

MAC FACT The TCP/IP Internet, which began some 20 years ago in the Defense Department's Defense Advanced Research Projects Agency (DARPA), is now a huge collection of hundreds of government, academic, and corporate networks—it includes millions of computers all over the world. In 1992, Apple created an AppleTalk Internet among several university and corporate sites across the United States. The AppleTalk Internet uses tunneling techniques through the much larger TCP/IP Internet in an effort to bring AppleTalk's ease of use to wide area public networking.

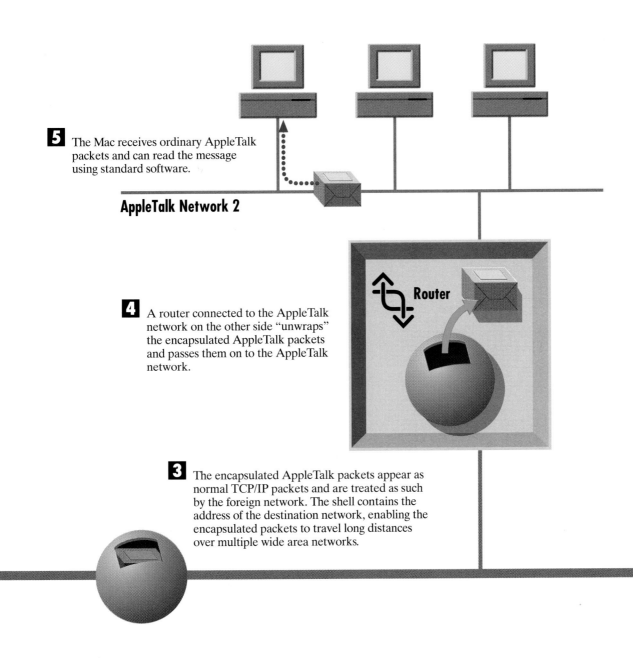

5 The Mac receives ordinary AppleTalk packets and can read the message using standard software.

AppleTalk Network 2

Router

4 A router connected to the AppleTalk network on the other side "unwraps" the encapsulated AppleTalk packets and passes them on to the AppleTalk network.

3 The encapsulated AppleTalk packets appear as normal TCP/IP packets and are treated as such by the foreign network. The shell contains the address of the destination network, enabling the encapsulated packets to travel long distances over multiple wide area networks.

PRINTING AND PUBLISHING

8

CONTENTS

ACCORDING TO *The American Heritage Dictionary*, the word *publish* is defined as the act of preparing and issuing of printed material for public distribution. In light of this definition, many of us are publishers in one way or another. The final result of our work on a Mac is often on paper, whether it's the 8½-by-11-inch memo to be distributed among our coworkers or a four-color illustrated brochure to be sent to clients. With paper still the preferred distribution medium of communicating information, the phrase "publish or perish" applies to more people than just college professors.

In 1984, Apple introduced two new pieces of hardware, the Macintosh and a printer. The ImageWriter I was the first Mac peripheral, preceding even the first hard-disk drive. This dot-matrix printer was noisy and slow, and it produced low-resolution printouts. Still, it and the new Macintosh computer had two big strong points—they made printing easy, and they could print graphics as easily as text. The installation procedure consisted of plugging in a cable between the two devices. It also used a single software printer driver for all applications; you could select it once and then print anything from any program.

As convenient as the ImageWriter was, the introduction of the LaserWriter the following year was a much bigger advance in printing technology, helping to start the desktop publishing revolution. The LaserWriter was the first network printer and one of the first laser printers for desktop computers. As such, it was quiet, could be accessed by multiple Mac users, and put quality text and graphics printing in the hands of ordinary users. The LaserWriter was also the first printer to use a page description language called PostScript, which made possible the scaling of type fonts to different sizes with acceptable results.

Desktop publishing and graphics are what made the Mac a successful machine in the mid-1980s. It was called desktop publishing because activities that were traditionally done by a roomful of people and thousands of dollars of equipment could now be done at your desk. Page layout software replaced the scissors and glue used to design a page of a newsletter or magazine and made revisions quick and easy. Electronic files replaced expensive and time-consuming photographic techniques, and the ability to include graphics right in the document file replaced the use of expensive stripping equipment.

Today, the Mac's built-in graphics and printing technologies and ease of setup and use make it a favorite among professional desktop publishers. The Mac is widely used by magazines and newspaper publishers, and it was used to create the graphics, text, and page layout of this book. However, the advances in desktop publishing technology over the last decade have put more demands on hardware and software, particularly with the use of color. One problem area is still the lack of calibration of color among different peripherals: What looks like burnt umber on one monitor is not necessarily the same shade on another monitor or on a color printer. Support for color calibration was added with the addition of ColorSync system software in 1992, which became part of QuickDraw GX the following year.

Of course, printing and publishing on the Mac is not all high-end color production. Laser printers still form the majority of printed output devices in use today. Dot-matrix printers like the ImageWriter have been mostly replaced by ink-jet printers, which are quieter and produce better results than their predecessors. We'll start our discussion of how desktop publishing and printing work with these two workhorses—ink-jet and laser printers.

PART EIGHT

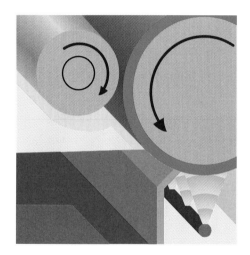

CHAPTER 30

How a Printer Works

LASER PRINTERS ARE ubiquitous office fixtures, now as common as copy machines. Though they vary in quality, speed, and cost, laser printers set the standards for these three printing parameters. Laser printers are available to fit the high-volume printing needs of big organizations, as well as the more modest requirements of the small workgroup and some individuals.

Ink-jet printers are popular because they are a great buy, offering low-cost printing with some of the print quality of laser printers. Ink-jet printers make great home printers, as they are almost silent in operation, small in size, and typically lightweight. Some are even portable and battery operated.

Most printers of all types create an image by drawing dots on paper. Standard printer resolution is 300 dots per inch, quite a bit higher than a monitor's 72 dots per inch, and higher resolutions are commonly available. An older technology, dot matrix, draws dots the same way typewriters create whole letters—by striking the paper through an inked ribbon. This makes dot-matrix printers useful for printing on forms that use carbon copies. Laser printers, on the other hand, are similar in design to copy machines. They use a dry powdered toner for the ink, which is applied electrostatically to the paper and bonded by heat. Ink-jet printers work the way the name implies, by squirting tiny jets of ink onto the paper.

Both laser and ink-jet printers come in color versions. Color printers work the same way their black-and-white counterparts do, except they print each page four times, one time each in cyan, magenta, yellow, and black ink. These colors combine to form all the other colors you need.

Color laser and ink-jet printers represent the lower end of color printing technology. Other types, such as wax-transfer and dye-sublimation printers, produce more realistic color images, but the costs of the printers and the printouts are much higher. The most expensive of these can produce color images indistinguishable from photographic prints.

Printers can either work over AppleTalk networks or be connected to a single Mac. Network laser printers have either LocalTalk or Ethernet connectors built in, and sometimes both. Typically, network laser printers use the PostScript page description language to print graphics and text. Nonnetwork laser or ink-jet printers are usually connected to a Mac's SCSI port or serial port and use the Mac's QuickDraw screen-drawing routines for printing.

Laser Printer

1 Printing commands that come in through an AppleTalk port are described by PostScript or TrueType. In non-network printers, the commands are from QuickDraw (see Chapter 24). The signals describing the document to be printed are sent to RAM on the printer's logic board for processing by the printer's CPU.

4 A laser beam is aimed at a rotating drum using a rotating polygonal mirror. The beam hits the drum one dot at a time. The laser is turned on where black dots will occur and is turned off where the page will remain white. Some printers use an array of light-emitting diodes instead of a laser. In standard printers, a black area will have 300 dots in every inch.

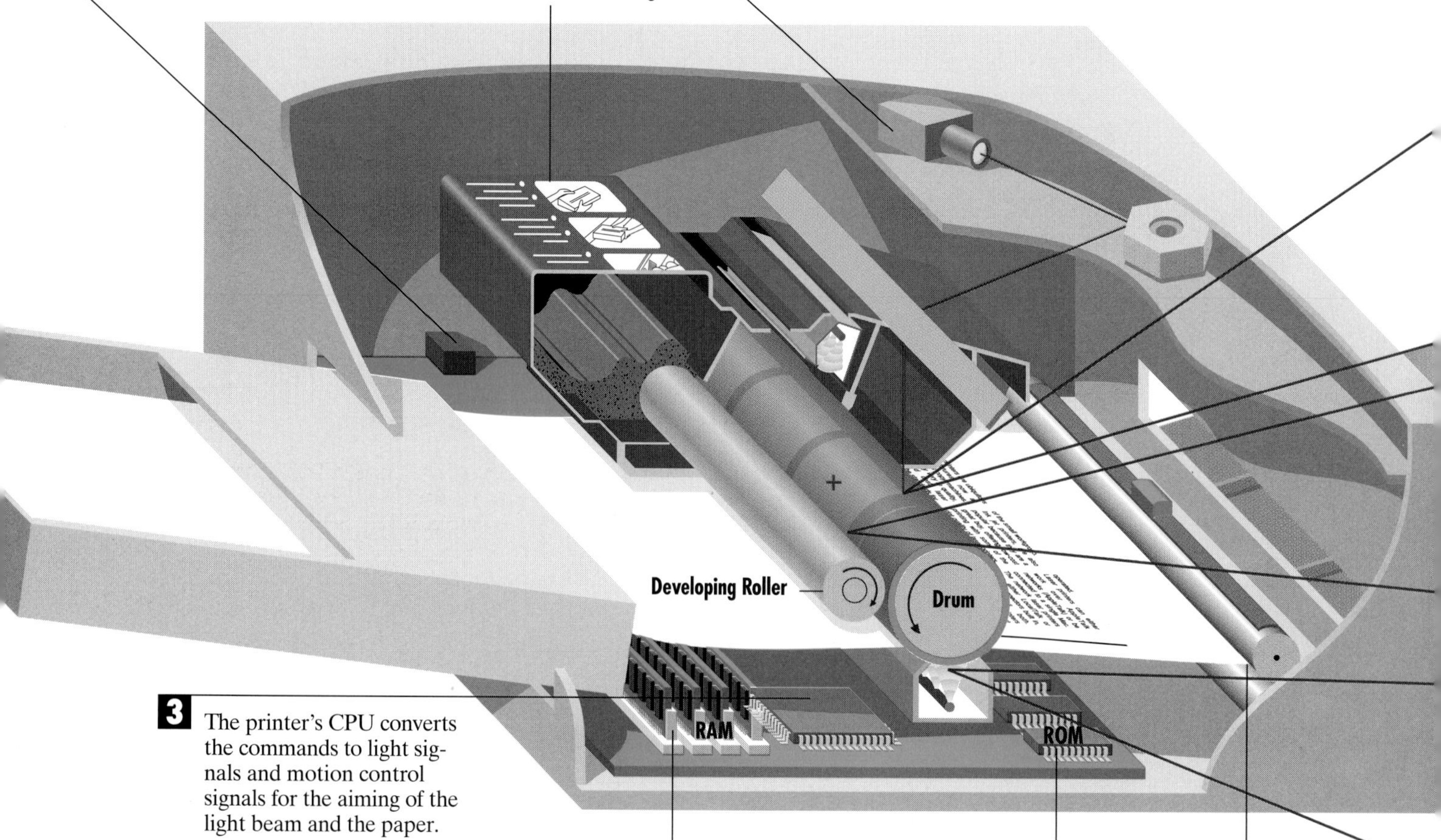

Toner Cartridge

Developing Roller

Drum

RAM

ROM

3 The printer's CPU converts the commands to light signals and motion control signals for the aiming of the light beam and the paper.

2 Part of the printing commands describes the fonts to be used in the document. Fonts are stored in the printer's ROM, in an external hard disk, or occasionally on a user's Mac. The requested fonts are loaded into RAM.

9 The toner is bonded to the paper by passing between two rollers heated to about 160 degrees centigrade.

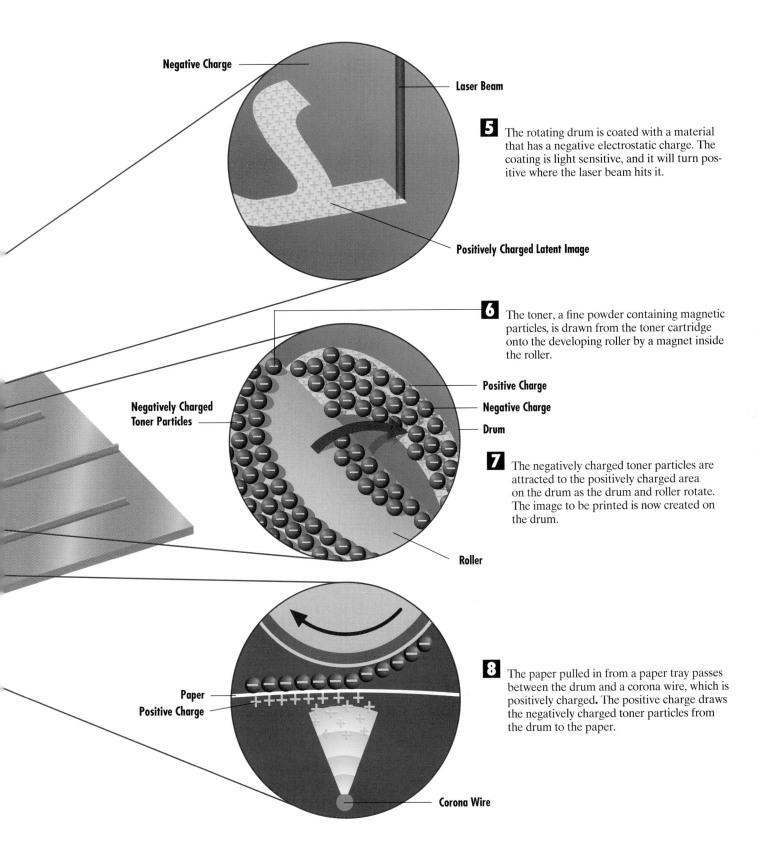

Negative Charge

Laser Beam

5 The rotating drum is coated with a material that has a negative electrostatic charge. The coating is light sensitive, and it will turn positive where the laser beam hits it.

Positively Charged Latent Image

6 The toner, a fine powder containing magnetic particles, is drawn from the toner cartridge onto the developing roller by a magnet inside the roller.

Positive Charge

Negative Charge

Drum

Negatively Charged Toner Particles

7 The negatively charged toner particles are attracted to the positively charged area on the drum as the drum and roller rotate. The image to be printed is now created on the drum.

Roller

Paper
Positive Charge

8 The paper pulled in from a paper tray passes between the drum and a corona wire, which is positively charged. The positive charge draws the negatively charged toner particles from the drum to the paper.

Corona Wire

Ink-Jet QuickDraw Printer

1 Unlike a PostScript laser printer, which processes the signals into a page image itself, a QuickDraw printer uses software on the Mac that intercepts QuickDraw commands going to the screen. The Mac processes the page image for printing and sends the finished data to the printer. The processed data for the first line is sent through a ribbon cable to the ink-cartridge-and-nozzle assembly.

5 The cartridge-and-nozzle assembly moves slightly to the right. After a line is written, the paper advances slightly and the cartridge-and-nozzle assembly moves back to the other side.

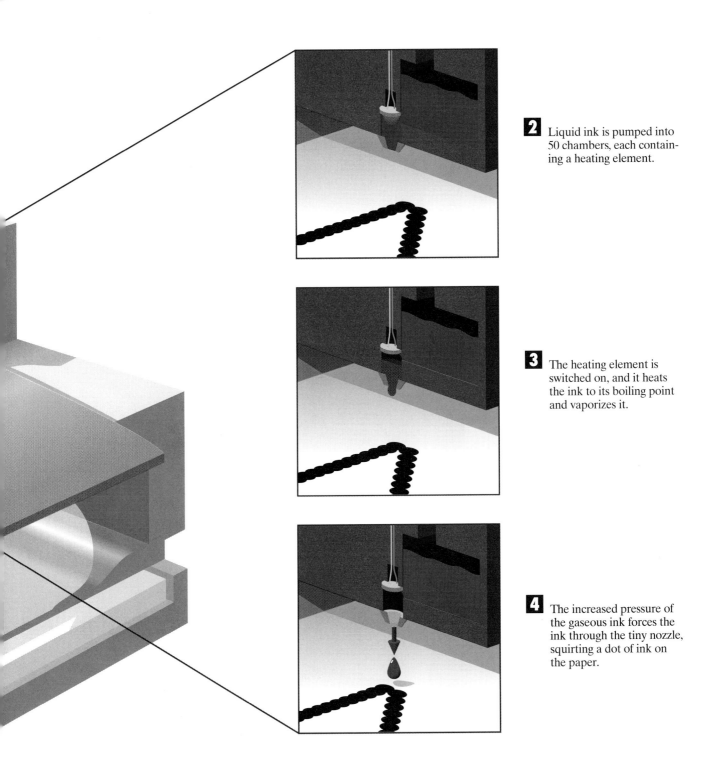

2 Liquid ink is pumped into 50 chambers, each containing a heating element.

3 The heating element is switched on, and it heats the ink to its boiling point and vaporizes it.

4 The increased pressure of the gaseous ink forces the ink through the tiny nozzle, squirting a dot of ink on the paper.

MAC FACT Nonnetwork ink-jet or laser printers connected to a Mac's serial port can be shared with other users on a network through printer-sharing software running on the Mac the printer is connected to. With some software, such Apple's GrayShare for the StyleWriter ink-jet printer, the Mac connected to the printer does the processing and will slow down when other users are accessing the printer. With Hewlett-Packard's software for the DeskJet ink-jet printer, the processing is done by the user's Mac, not by the Mac the printer is connected to.

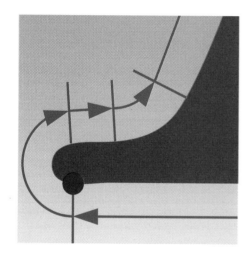

How PostScript Works

PRINTERS AND MACS speak different languages. When you print a file, you're not actually sending the file itself to the printer, you're sending a description of what's on the pages in a language the printer can understand.

You could send printers a bitmapped representation, which is a dot-by-dot account of what's on the page. This is how the Mac prints to QuickDraw printers, such as 1984's dot-matrix ImageWriter and today's ink-jet printers. However, bitmapped printing moves a large amount of data over cables, which presents a problem on networks. You also have to teach the Mac how to talk to each different printer you use.

In 1985, Adobe Systems Incorporated introduced the PostScript page description language on the Apple LaserWriter. Since then it has been a standard method of telling printers what to print. Instead of describing each dot, PostScript describes everything in a document—including text, fonts, style, shapes, fills, and colors—mathematically. It draws the dots on the paper after the description of the file has been transmitted, not before. This is a much more efficient way of describing a document, requiring the transmission of much less data over the cables and producing more consistent results. PostScript is also printer independent because it describes text and graphics in a mathematical manner. PostScript sends its commands in a format that all devices can understand—ASCII (American Standard Code for Information Interchange) text.

PostScript's fonts are called *outline fonts* because the outline of each character is used to draw each type of character. Outline fonts are usually stored in the printer. Most professional desktop publishers prefer to use Adobe's Type 1 fonts, but other vendors sell fonts, called PostScript clones, that work with PostScript printers. There are also non-PostScript outline fonts that you can use, the most prevalent being TrueType, which works similarly to PostScript fonts. Another language, Hewlett-Packard's Page Printer Command Language, is used by IBM-compatible PCs, but rarely by Macs.

In the early 1990s Adobe released an extension to its page description language called Postscript Level 2, which adds new features, such as the ability to select paper trays from your Mac. PostScript Level 2, implemented in newer printers, can also do everything Level 1 can.

PostScript Printing

1 When you print a document to a PostScript printer, the application creates a small program called a *page description* (also called a print job), which will be executed by the printer. The page description contains a set of print commands written in the PostScript page description language; these commands treat the entire document as a single graphic. The commands describe graphic objects, such as lines, curves, circles, and squares, and more complex objects made up of these elements. They also describe scanned graphics, such as photographs. The page description contains all the characters in the document and the names of the fonts and styles used. The commands describe where on the page to draw characters and graphics, as well as their sizes, colors, and other attributes.

2 The page description is sent over the network to the printer as ASCII text. Sending a list of commands is much more efficient and requires less code than describing the location and color of each pixel on the page, the way that monitors and QuickDraw printers do. Using ASCII allows any PostScript printer or device to understand the characters contained in the code.

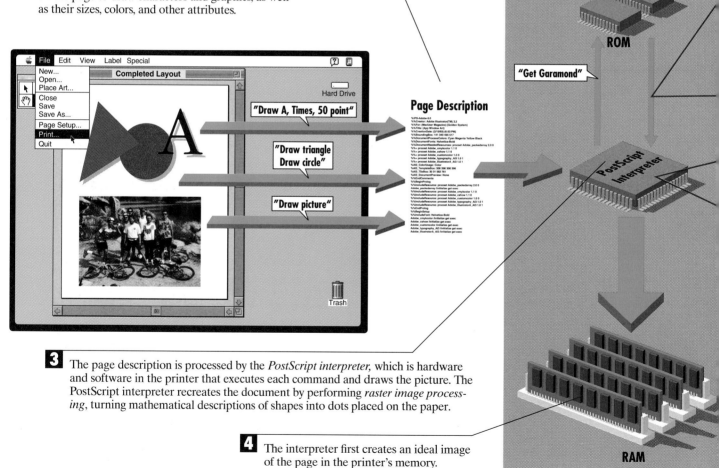

Page Description

PostScript Printer

ROM

"Get Garamond"

PostScript Interpreter

RAM

"Draw A, Times, 50 point"

"Draw triangle
Draw circle"

"Draw picture"

3 The page description is processed by the *PostScript interpreter*, which is hardware and software in the printer that executes each command and draws the picture. The PostScript interpreter recreates the document by performing *raster image processing*, turning mathematical descriptions of shapes into dots placed on the paper.

4 The interpreter first creates an ideal image of the page in the printer's memory.

MAC FACT Although applications create PostScript page descriptions automatically, PostScript is also a programming language that can be used to create special print effects not included in your applications—presuming you know the language. To get a look at PostScript code, many applications let you create a file containing all the PostScript code for a particular document. Usually, you create a file of PostScript code by clicking a button in the Print dialog box: Instead of sending a page description to a printer, the application saves it to your hard disk.

5 When the page description commands specify the use of a particular font, the PostScript interpreter fetches the font stored in the printer's ROM, hard disk, or RAM if the font is downloaded from the Mac. PostScript uses its own set of outline fonts, each of which is a set of mathematical descriptions of characters. PostScript fonts are shapes, which are treated as graphical objects.

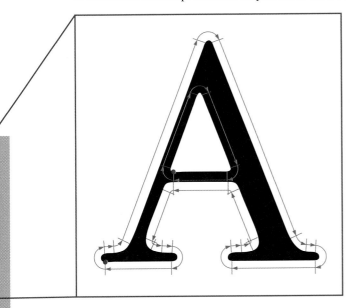

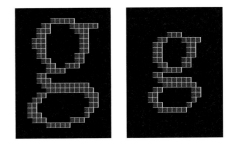

6 Because PostScript fonts are smooth outlines described mathematically, a character is shaped the same in any font size. Bitmapped fonts, on the other hand, are not scalable, and the character looks different at each size.

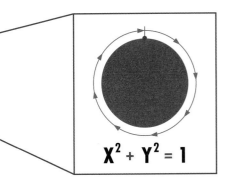

$$X^2 + Y^2 = 1$$

7 When the interpreter receives a command such as "draw a circle," it creates the path of the shape's outline using a simple mathematical equation. The outlines of more complex shapes are described by many mathematical equations and geometric relationships. Page description commands tell the interpreter the thickness of the outline and the colors (for a color printer) of the fill pattern.

9 Color printers mix dots of cyan, magenta, yellow, and black in different proportions to approximate colors; this is called *dithering*. For creating gray-scale images, such as photographs, on printers that can only print black and white, the interpreter also uses dithering to produce approximations of grays called halftones. Dithering mixes dots of black and white in different amounts to appear as shades of gray. Newspaper publishers use dithering to produce gray-scale and color photos.

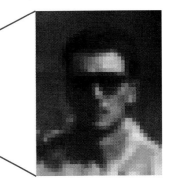

8 With the document image recreated in printer RAM, the interpreter tells the printing mechanism to print dots of toner on the paper. The number of dots per inch depends on the resolution and settings of the printer; the same page description code could produce 300 dots per inch on one printer and 1,000 on another. The resolution of the printout is completely independent of the monitor resolution.

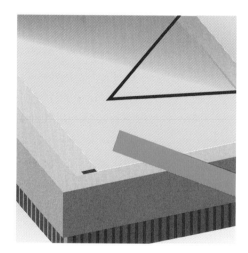

How Color Matching Works

BLACK-AND-WHITE desktop publishing is fairly straightforward as far as input and output go—what you see on your screen is basically what the printer produces. Add color, and everything changes, as users learned when quality color printers and scanners first began to arrive on the desktop publishing scene. People discovered that when you scan in a photograph, the colors you see on screen or that the printer produces bear little resemblance to the original. This is because scanners, monitors, and printers all treat color differently, varying from model to model. To cope with the problem, Apple introduced ColorSync, system software for color matching that converts the different ways devices describe color.

To understand how color matching works, it's helpful to understand a little about how color works. Color is a not a property of physics; it is completely a phenomenon of the eye and brain. Receptors in the eyes react to a narrow band of wavelengths of electromagnetic radiation called *visible light*, and the brain turns signals from the eyes into colors. The range of visible light starts with violet at 380 mμ (millimicrons, or millionths of a millimeter) and goes to red at 780 mμ. Radiation with shorter wavelengths is called ultraviolet, followed by microwaves, X rays, gamma rays, and cosmic rays. Radiation with longer wavelengths is called infrared, followed by radar waves, radio waves, and television waves.

Sunlight, as Isaac Newton first demonstrated in 1676, is a mixture of all wavelengths of visible light. We see an object, such as grass, as having a color because it reflects certain wavelengths, which we see and absorbs other wavelengths, which we don't see. Most natural colors we see are not a single wavelength. For instance, green grass may reflect light at all frequencies in varying amounts, not just 540 mμ, which is the wavelength we associate with green. However, specifying all the wavelengths reflected by an object is so complex that computer devices use other ways to describe color.

As you saw in Chapter 24, you only need three colors to represent any other color. The Mac uses the red, green, and blue (RGB) model to display colors on a monitor. A color created this way may not use all the wavelengths of light reflected by the original object, but it is close enough for the eye. The problem with color models like RGB is that they are device dependent; they don't really describe color, they only approximate it. Also, different devices often use different color models. Color printers typically use some type of CMYK (cyan, magenta, yellow, and black) model for mixing inks on a page.

Scanners, monitors, and printers also have different *gamuts*, the range of colors they can reproduce. Since monitors have the widest gamuts, there are colors specified for display on a monitor that can't be reproduced using a printer's color model.

Color matching systems calibrate computer devices to a standard, device-independent color model, and they use this standard to match the colors produced by different color models and gamuts. The most common device-independent color model is the XYZ model created by the Commission International de l'Eclairage (CIE) in 1931. The CIE XYZ color model is not based on any theory of color (and there are many), but rather on purely experimental data gathered from standard light sources and from averaging what actual observers reported seeing. The CIE XYZ model is a mathematically complex description of color. It is not used to produce colors because it would take much more computing power than the simpler color models used by today's computer equipment. However, it is useful as a standard by which to compare different systems.

ColorSync is built into QuickDraw GX and is also available separately. ColorSync is a system-level framework that can do color matching itself or enable an add-in matching system from a third party. ColorSync is therefore flexible and extensible, open to innovations in color matching that may come along in the future.

ColorSync Color Matching

ColorSync manages the matching of colors between scanners, monitors, and printers by comparing the description of a color by each system to the standard CIE XYZ color model. It doesn't actually alter the electronic file being passed from scanner to printer. Scanners and monitors describe a color using three numbers that represent the amounts of red, green, and blue (or hue, saturation, and brightness) in the resulting color. Printers use four numbers that represent the amounts of cyan, magenta, yellow, and black ink used to create a color. However, each device can only create a subset of the colors described in the standard CIE XYZ system.

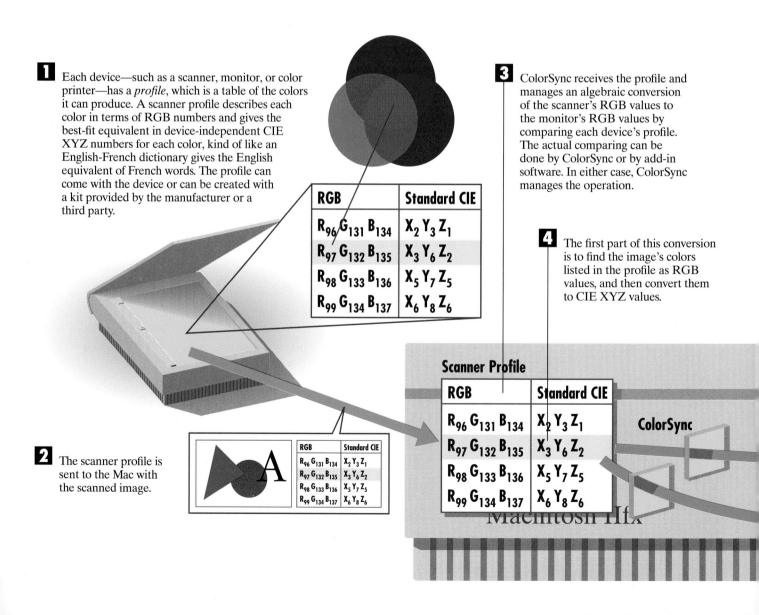

1 Each device—such as a scanner, monitor, or color printer—has a *profile*, which is a table of the colors it can produce. A scanner profile describes each color in terms of RGB numbers and gives the best-fit equivalent in device-independent CIE XYZ numbers for each color, kind of like an English-French dictionary gives the English equivalent of French words. The profile can come with the device or can be created with a kit provided by the manufacturer or a third party.

RGB	Standard CIE
$R_{96} G_{131} B_{134}$	$X_2 Y_3 Z_1$
$R_{97} G_{132} B_{135}$	$X_3 Y_6 Z_2$
$R_{98} G_{133} B_{136}$	$X_5 Y_7 Z_5$
$R_{99} G_{134} B_{137}$	$X_6 Y_8 Z_6$

3 ColorSync receives the profile and manages an algebraic conversion of the scanner's RGB values to the monitor's RGB values by comparing each device's profile. The actual comparing can be done by ColorSync or by add-in software. In either case, ColorSync manages the operation.

4 The first part of this conversion is to find the image's colors listed in the profile as RGB values, and then convert them to CIE XYZ values.

2 The scanner profile is sent to the Mac with the scanned image.

RGB	Standard CIE
$R_{96} G_{131} B_{134}$	$X_2 Y_3 Z_1$
$R_{97} G_{132} B_{135}$	$X_3 Y_6 Z_2$
$R_{98} G_{133} B_{136}$	$X_5 Y_7 Z_5$
$R_{99} G_{134} B_{137}$	$X_6 Y_8 Z_6$

Scanner Profile

RGB	Standard CIE
$R_{96} G_{131} B_{134}$	$X_2 Y_3 Z_1$
$R_{97} G_{132} B_{135}$	$X_3 Y_6 Z_2$
$R_{98} G_{133} B_{136}$	$X_5 Y_7 Z_5$
$R_{99} G_{134} B_{137}$	$X_6 Y_8 Z_6$

ColorSync

Macintosh IIfx

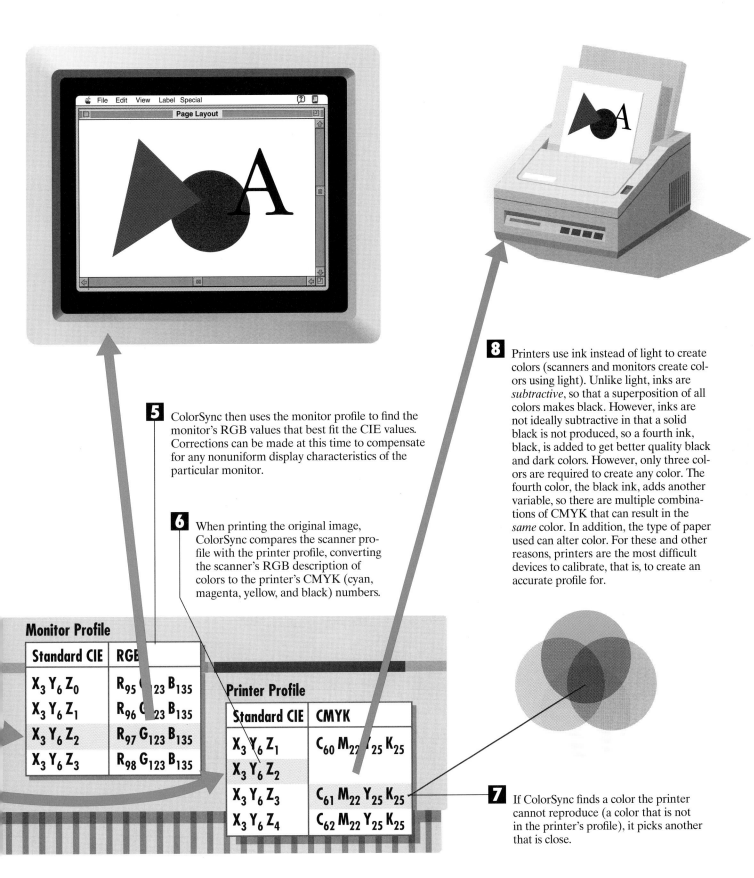

8 Printers use ink instead of light to create colors (scanners and monitors create colors using light). Unlike light, inks are *subtractive*, so that a superposition of all colors makes black. However, inks are not ideally subtractive in that a solid black is not produced, so a fourth ink, black, is added to get better quality black and dark colors. However, only three colors are required to create any color. The fourth color, the black ink, adds another variable, so there are multiple combinations of CMYK that can result in the *same* color. In addition, the type of paper used can alter color. For these and other reasons, printers are the most difficult devices to calibrate, that is, to create an accurate profile for.

5 ColorSync then uses the monitor profile to find the monitor's RGB values that best fit the CIE values. Corrections can be made at this time to compensate for any nonuniform display characteristics of the particular monitor.

6 When printing the original image, ColorSync compares the scanner profile with the printer profile, converting the scanner's RGB description of colors to the printer's CMYK (cyan, magenta, yellow, and black) numbers.

Monitor Profile

Standard CIE	RGB
$X_3 Y_6 Z_0$	$R_{95} G_{123} B_{135}$
$X_3 Y_6 Z_1$	$R_{96} G_{123} B_{135}$
$X_3 Y_6 Z_2$	$R_{97} G_{123} B_{135}$
$X_3 Y_6 Z_3$	$R_{98} G_{123} B_{135}$

Printer Profile

Standard CIE	CMYK
$X_3 Y_6 Z_1$	$C_{60} M_{22} Y_{25} K_{25}$
$X_3 Y_6 Z_2$	
$X_3 Y_6 Z_3$	$C_{61} M_{22} Y_{25} K_{25}$
$X_3 Y_6 Z_4$	$C_{62} M_{22} Y_{25} K_{25}$

7 If ColorSync finds a color the printer cannot reproduce (a color that is not in the printer's profile), it picks another that is close.

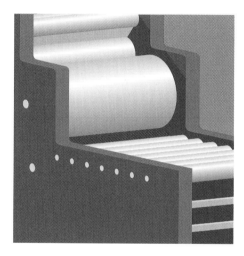

How Desktop Publishing Works

DESKTOP PUBLISHING WAS born on the Macintosh. It was not something Apple invented, but grew out of a need to make publishing easier. The Mac supplied the first tools to put out a newsletter or brochure from your desk, tools that replaced the scissors and glue of page layout—formerly known as paste up—as well as the hundred-thousand-dollar machinery required for graphics. By reducing costs, making revisions easier, and making publications look better, the Mac put publishing in the hands of the individual and streamlined the empires of the publishing industry.

In the professional publishing industry, the Mac is the favorite desktop publishing platform, mostly because its integrated design makes it more versatile and easier to set up and learn than other platforms. Macs are used to put out newspapers and magazines all over the country. Even magazines covering IBM PCs and Microsoft Windows use Macs in their production departments. This book was produced entirely on Macs. Of course, desktop publishing isn't limited to book and magazine publishers. The result of your work can be a color brochure, an eight-page newsletter, or an 8½-by-11-inch sheet of paper.

At the heart of desktop publishing is page layout software, which allows you to manipulate text and illustrations on a page. Page layout software has grown increasingly powerful, allowing detailed adjustments in the spacing of individual characters, as well as graphics editing. Today, you have a wide selection of page layout programs to choose from, and you can even do page layout in some powerful word processors.

Placing a color illustration in a document was once costly and time-consuming. Not only is this an easy task with desktop publishing, but now a skilled artist can create the illustrations on the Mac. The possible styles range from simple informational graphics used in newspapers, to drawings that look like they were created with chalk and ink, to realistic, three-dimensional renderings.

Desktop publishing has been fully integrated in the production process all the way through professional printing. In most service bureaus, Macs control the process of color separation, a production step before color printing. With the advent of the RISC-based PowerPC, Macs will have an even greater role in the publishing world.

Desktop Publishing

4 The electronic files are sent to a Mac running a page layout program. The files can be sent over a network or a telephone link, or they can be transported on floppy disks or other removable media.

1 A writer creates the text of the document in a word processor. A full-featured word processor can be used as a page layout program for less complex documents.

2 Artists use drawing or painting software to create illustrations (such as the ones in this book) as well as decorative elements on a page.

3 A scanner electronically captures images of photographs or other art. A flatbed scanner is typically used to capture photographs or images from books, though a slide scanner can be used for capturing 35 mm slides.

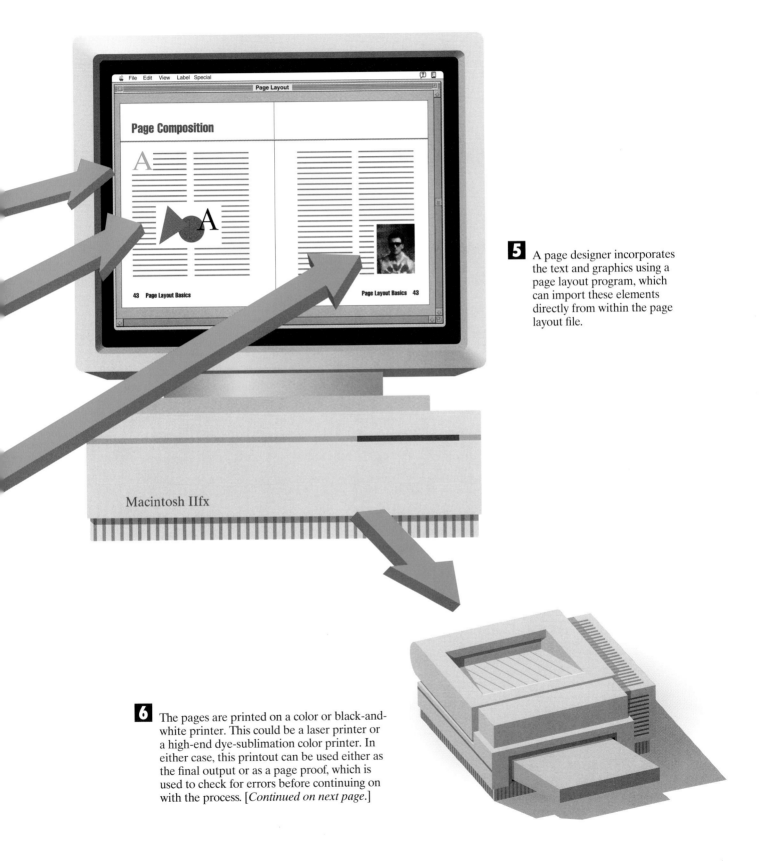

Page Composition

43   Page Layout Basics

Page Layout Basics   43

5 A page designer incorporates the text and graphics using a page layout program, which can import these elements directly from within the page layout file.

Macintosh IIfx

6 The pages are printed on a color or black-and-white printer. This could be a laser printer or a high-end dye-sublimation color printer. In either case, this printout can be used either as the final output or as a page proof, which is used to check for errors before continuing on with the process. [*Continued on next page.*]

Desktop Publishing

Service Bureau

9 Color separation software on the Mac produces four electronic documents, each representing the amount of cyan, magenta, yellow, and black (or CMYK) that will go on the page.

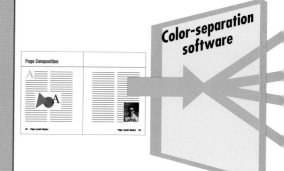

Color-separation software

Portable data storage

7 When printing on a printing press, the page layout file is sent to a service bureau, typically by mail or courier—the amount of data is usually too large to make modem transfer practical. At the service bureau, the page layout file is loaded onto a high-end Mac.

8 Images scanned on flatbed scanners are usually of lower resolution than required for high-end desktop publishing. Production software on the Mac automatically strips out scanned images and replaces them with images that have been rescanned with a high-resolution drum scanner.

High-resolution scanner

MAC FACT At 5:04 p.m. on October 17, 1989, an earthquake of magnitude 6.9 on the Richter scale brought the San Francisco Bay Area to a grinding halt. Power and telephone service were out for days in some locations and for months in others, shutting down most TV and radio stations. Despite the disruptions, the *San Francisco Chronicle* was able to publish an edition the very next morning, a mere 12 hours after the earthquake, through the use of a small generator and several Macintoshes.

10 The four electronic documents are fed into an imagesetter, which produces four full-sized transparent negatives (the white area of a page is black, and black text is white). Although there is one negative each for cyan, magenta, yellow, and black, the negatives themselves are in gray scale, not color. If you lay the four transparencies on top of each other, you get an accurate gray-scale negative of the whole page.

11 The color separation negatives are used to make flexible plates for the printing press, one ink color per plate. A clear area on the film becomes a solid raised area on the plate, which will let all the color get printed on the paper. A gray area on the film becomes an area of raised dots on the plate, which will put down a limited amount of ink on the paper. A black area results in no raised area and nothing for the ink to stick to, leaving the paper white. The plates are attached to four rollers on the printing press, one for each color. As the paper passes under each roller, it gets a coat of one of the four colors.

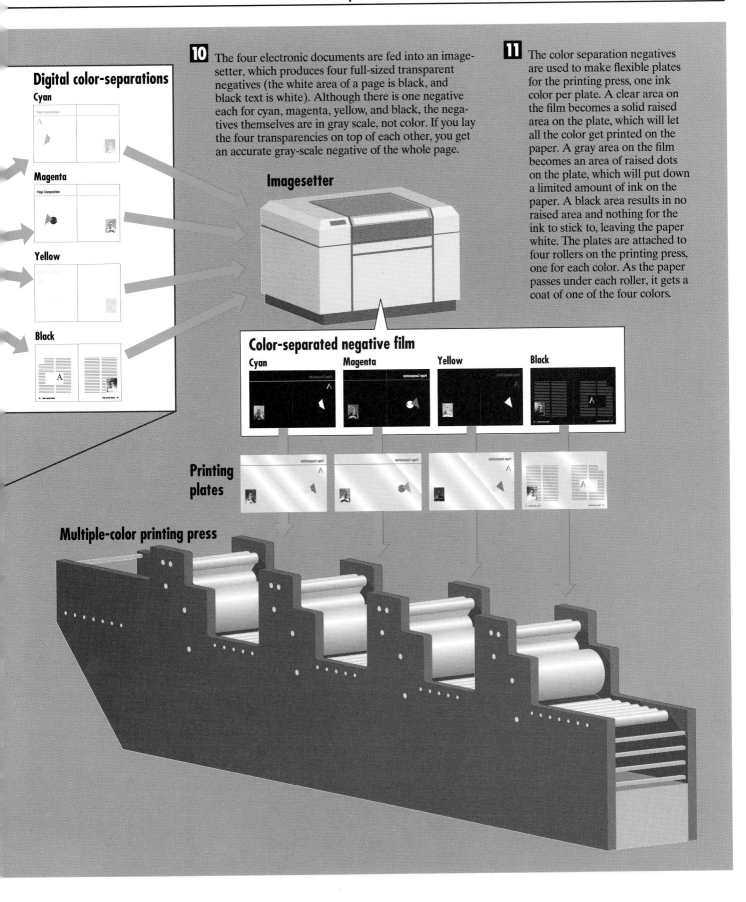

Digital color-separations

Cyan

Magenta

Yellow

Black

Imagesetter

Color-separated negative film

Cyan   Magenta   Yellow   Black

Printing plates

Multiple-color printing press

Imagination.
Innovation. Insight.

The How It Works Series from Ziff-Davis Press

"... a magnificently seamless integration of text and graphics ..."

Larry Blasko, The Associated Press, reviewing *PC/Computing How Computers Work*

No other books bring computer technology to life like the *How It Works* series from Ziff-Davis Press.

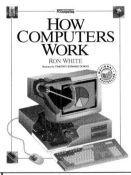

HOW COMPUTERS WORK
RON WHITE

ISBN: 094-7 Price: $22.95

Lavish, full-color illustrations and lucid text from some of the world's top computer commentators make *How It Works* books an exciting way to explore the inner workings of PC technology.

PC/Computing How Computers Work

A worldwide blockbuster that hit the general trade bestseller lists! *PC/Computing* magazine executive editor Ron White dismantles the PC and reveals what really makes it tick.

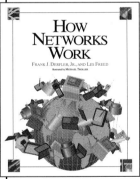

HOW NETWORKS WORK
FRANK J. DERFLER, JR., AND LES FREED

ISBN: 129-3 Price: $24.95

How Networks Work

Two of the most respected names in connectivity showcase the PC network, illustrating and explaining how each component does its magic and how they all fit together.

ALL ABOUT COMPUTERS
JEAN ATELSEK

ISBN: 166-8 Price: $15.95
Available: October

How Macs Work

A fun and fascinating voyage to the heart of the Macintosh! Two noted *MacUser* contributors cover the spectrum of Macintosh operations from startup to shutdown.

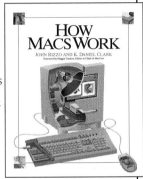

HOW MACS WORK
JOHN RIZZO AND K. DANIEL CLARK

ISBN: 146-3 Price: $24.95

How Software Works

This dazzlingly illustrated volume from Ron White peeks inside the PC to show in full-color detail how software breathes life into the PC. Covers all major software categories.

Note:

HOW SOFTWARE WORKS
RON WHITE

ISBN: 133-1 Price: $24.95
Available: October

How to Use Your Computer

Conquer computerphobia and see how this intricate machine truly makes life easier. Dozens of full-color graphics showcase the components of the PC and explain how to interact with them.

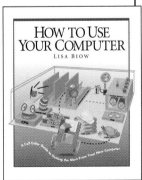

HOW TO USE YOUR COMPUTER
LISA BIOW

ISBN: 155-2 Price: $19.95
Available: September

All About Computers

This one-of-a-kind visual guide for kids features numerous full-color illustrations and photos on every page, combined with dozens of interactive projects that reinforce computer basics, making this an exciting way to learn all about the world of computers.

© 1993 Ziff-Davis Press

ZIFF-DAVIS
ZD PRESS

Available at all fine bookstores or by calling 1-800-688-0448, ext. 100.

Attention Teachers and Trainers

NOW YOU CAN TEACH FROM THIS BOOK!

ZD Press now offers instructors and trainers the materials they need to use this book in their classes.

- An Instructor's Manual features flexible lessons designed for use in a 10- or 15-week course (30-45 course hours).

- Student exercises and tests on floppy disk provide you with an easy way to tailor and/or duplicate tests as you need them.

- A Transparency Package contains all the graphics from the book, each on a single, full-color transparency.

These materials are available only to qualified accounts.
For more information contact:

In the U.S.A:
Academic Institutions: Suzanne Anthony, 800-786-6541
Corporations, Government Agencies: Cindy Johnson, 800-488-8741
In Canada: Copp Clark Pitman Ltd.
In the U.K.: The Computer Bookshops
In Australia: WoodLane Pty. Ltd.